Civil War Acoustic Shadows

By
Charles D. Ross

WHITE MANE BOOKS
SHIPPENSBURG, PENNSYLVANIA

Original diagrams drawn by John M. Early.

This White Mane Books publication
was printed by
Beidel Printing House, Inc.
63 West Burd Street
Shippensburg, PA 17257-0152 USA

The acid-free paper used in this book meets the guidelines for permanence and durability of the Committee on Production Guidelines for Book Longevity of the Council on Library Resources.

For a complete list of available publications
please write
White Mane Books
Division of White Mane Publishing Company, Inc.
P.O. Box 152
Shippensburg, PA 17257-0152 USA

Library of Congress Cataloging-in-Publication Data

Ross, Charles D., 1958-
    Civil War acoustic shadows / by Charles D. Ross.
        p. cm.
    Includes bibliographical references and index.
    ISBN 1-57249-254-6 (alk. paper)
    1. United States--History--Civil War, 1861-1865--Campaigns. 2. Battles--United States--Noise--History--19th century. 3. Noise--Social aspects--United States--History--19th century. 4. Noise--United States--Psychological aspects--History--19th century. 5. Generals--United States--History--19th century. 6. Command of troops--History--19th century. I. Title.

E470 .R67 2001
973.7'3--dc21

                                                    2001017778

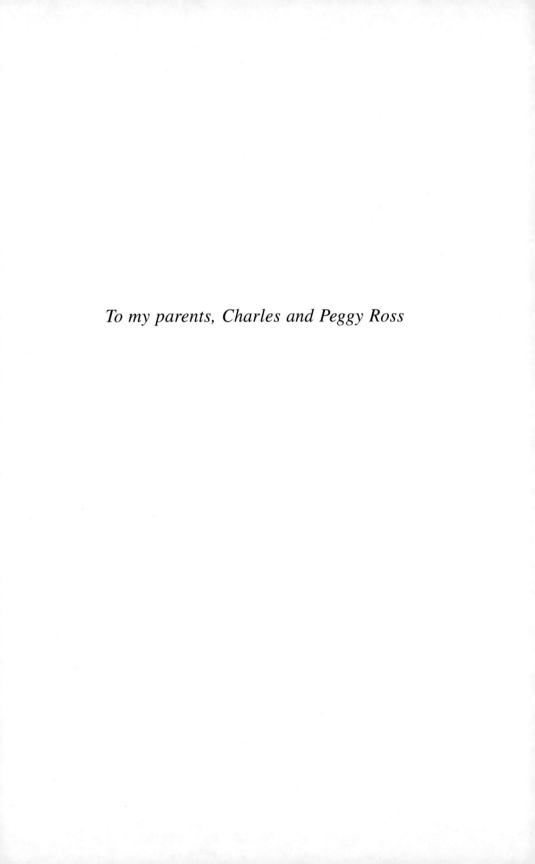

To my parents, Charles and Peggy Ross

Contents

Illustrations

Chapter 1

A Curious Occurrence at Gaines's Mill

On June 27, 1862, two men rode side by side through the gently undulating countryside just to the northeast of Richmond, Virginia. They had come to witness a battle that would be the most violent conflict ever seen in America up to that time.

Confederate forces, most fighting for the first time under the command of General Robert E. Lee, struck hard at the Union army perched on a hilltop near Gaines's Mill. Along with a heavy skirmish the afternoon before at Beaver Dam, the battle of Gaines's Mill marked the beginning of what would later be called the Seven Days' Battles. It was the beginning of the Lee legend, as the outnumbered Confederates pushed George McClellan's Federals back to the James River and finally all the way to Maryland.

Gaines's Mill was a ferocious fight, with the Confederates making one unsuccessful assault after another across Boatswain's Swamp and up the hill at the Yankees. Both lines were somewhat U-shaped, with the Confederate troops wrapped around the Union's interior lines. Cannonballs, canister, and bullets were flying in almost every direction. The fighting started in early afternoon and when the Confederates finally carried the Union position, five hours of nonstop killing had passed.

The battle was not the biggest of the Civil War, but it must have been remarkably loud. A great number of those involved in the battle (many of whom would later fight at Antietam, Gettysburg and the Wilderness) retained the memory of the incredible intensity of the sounds of weaponry on each side. Douglas Southall Freeman, biographer of

Robert E. Lee, said that Gaines's Mill was the noisiest of all the Seven Days' battles and adds that many veterans later said that it was "the most appalling in its din of any combat of the war."[1]

Major General Fitz John Porter, in command of the Union forces on the field, wrote: "The fierce firing of artillery and infantry, the crash of the shot, the bursting of shells, and the whizzing of bullets heard above the roar of artillery and the volleys of musketry, all combined, was something fearful."[2] Major General A. P. Hill, commanding a Confederate division, wrote in his official report that "The incessant roar of musketry and deep thunder of artillery told that the whole force of the enemy was in my front."[3]

Heros von Borke, a Prussian who had volunteered and become a colonel in the Confederate cavalry, remarked later: "The fire of musketry called continuously, and more than 150 howitzers and Napoleon and Parrot guns opened all around us and united in one incessant roar."[4]

Like other battles early in the Civil War, this battle (despite its violence) was seen by a number of spectators. The two riders mentioned above were Confederate Secretary of War George Wythe Randolph and Robert Garlick Hill Kean, a member of Randolph's staff. As they watched the battle from a hillside about a mile and a half from the main action, they noticed a most unusual phenomenon. Kean later described his observations in a letter to the British scientist John Tyndall:[5]

> Lynchburg, Virginia, *March* 19, 1874.
>
> Sir: I have just read with great interest your lecture of January 16th, on the acoustic transparency and opacity of the atmosphere. The remarkable observations you mention induce me to state to you a fact which I have occasionally mentioned, but always, where I am not well known, with the apprehension that my veracity would be questioned. It made a strong impression on me at the time, but was an insoluble mystery until your discourse gave me a possible solution.
>
> On the afternoon of June 28, 1862 [*sic*], I rode, in company with General G. W. Randolph, then Secretary of War of the Confederate States, to Price's house, about nine miles from Richmond; the evening before General Lee had begun his attack on McClellan's

army, by crossing the Chickahominy about four miles above Price's, and by driving in McClellan's right wing. The battle of Gaines's Farm was fought the afternoon to which I refer. The valley of the Chickahominy is about one and a half miles wide from hill-top to hill-top. Price's is on one hill-top, that nearest to Richmond; Gaines's farm, just opposite, is on the other, reaching back in a plateau to Cold Harbor.

Looking across the valley I saw a good deal of the battle, Lee's right resting in the valley, the Federal left wing the same. My line of vision was nearly in the line of the lines of battle. I saw the advance of the Confederates, their repulse two or three times, and in the gray of the evening the final retreat of the Federal forces.

I distinctly saw the musket-fire of both lines, the smoke, individual discharges, the flash of the guns. I saw batteries of artillery on both sides come into action and fire rapidly. Several field-batteries on each side were plainly in sight. Many more were hid by the timber which bounded the range of vision.

Yet looking for nearly two hours, from about 5 to 7 P.M. on a midsummer afternoon, at a battle in which at least 50,000 men were actually engaged, and doubtless at least 100 pieces of field-artillery, through an atmosphere optically as limpid as possible, *not a single sound of the battle* was audible to General Randolph and myself. I remarked it to him at the time as astonishing.

Between me and the battle was the deep broad valley of the Chickahominy, partly a swamp shaded from the declining sun by the hills and forest in the west (my side). Part of the valley on each side of the swamp was cleared; some in cultivation, some not. Here were conditions capable of providing several belts of air, varying in the amount of watery vapor (and probably in temperature), arranged like laminae at right angles to the acoustic waves as they came from the battle-field to me.

Respectfully,

Your obedient servant,

R.G.H. Kean

Here is an observation that on first glance appears to be hallucinatory. How could anyone within plain sight of a violent battle not hear its sounds? It seems too fantastic to be true. Randolph and Kean, though serving in civilian positions, had both been in military service earlier in the war. Randolph had been lauded as something of a hero for his work as an artillery commander at the battles of Big Bethel and First Manassas the previous year. Surely he must have been at least as astonished as Kean by the silence.

Kean's account is supported, though, by an observation by an experienced Union officer nearby. Troops under Brigadier General W. F. Smith (who, in turn, was under Major General William B. Franklin, commanding the Federal VI Corps) were involved in a side action (known as The Action at Golding's [or Garnett's] Farm) near the main battlefield of Gaines's Mill. Franklin later wrote: "The position held by General Smith's division was about one and one-half miles from Gaines's Mill field; and, possibly because the interval was filled with dense timber, not a gun of the Gaines's Mill battle was heard by the troops in our vicinity."

Well-known Civil War author Stephen Sears writes: "Normally the sound of artillery at that distance was easily heard, but on this hot and sultry day there would be acoustic shadows, like that at Seven Pines, scattered all across the field. Little of the Gaines's Mill fighting would be heard at McClellan's headquarters at the Trent house just across the river, for example…"[6]

Confederate Brigadier General Evander M. Law wrote in 1887: "To the troops stationed near the river, on the Richmond side, the action at Gaines's Mill was plainly visible, that part of it, at least, which took place in the open ground. I have been told by an eye-witness that from Price's house, on the opposite side, he could distinctly see the Confederate lines advancing to the attack through the open ground beyond the Chickahominy swamp, and could distinguish the direction of the lines of battle by the volume of smoke arising from the woods farther to the Confederate center and left. But it was all like a pantomime; not a sound could be heard, neither the tremendous roar of the musketry nor even the reports of the artillery. As they saw our assaulting lines recoil from the onset, as they were several times compelled to do early in the fight, the anxiety of our friend's 'over the river' to help was intense; but the enemy was in their front also, and their time for action would soon come."[7]

As Kean states in his letter, he was struck by the events of the day but often reluctant to discuss them because of the bizarre nature of what he had experienced. His letter to Tyndall was prompted by his reading of Tyndall's lecture notes regarding phenomena very similar to what Kean had seen at Gaines's Mill.

Tyndall in turn may have been led into an investigation of the phenomena to some extent by his knowledge that history had seen other "silent battles." As we shall see, "silent battles" and "acoustic shadows" had happened before and have happened since that hot Virginia day.

Furthermore, both Kean and Tyndall appear to have been unaware that there were some other strange acoustics associated with Gaines's Mill. A letter in the *Richmond Dispatch* of August 13, 1862, states that the sounds of the battle were heard in Staunton (about one hundred ten miles west of Gaines's Mill), and the artillery was even noted in McDowell, 35 miles farther west. Another letter (this in the *Richmond Examiner* of July 2, 1862) states that the noise of battle was heard in Peaks of Otter, about one hundred forty miles west of Gaines's Mill. The battle's fury, however, apparently completely missed Beaver Dam in Hanover County, just 25 miles west of the battlefield.[8]

Could there be any truth in these letters? Can the sounds of a battle be heard clearly over one hundred miles from the scene, but not at a point much closer? The answer is an emphatic "yes." This unusual audibility at long range has been noted for centuries.

As interesting as the acoustic events associated with Gaines's Mill were and are, they appear to have had no bearing on the outcome of the battle. The men involved in the fighting and killing apparently had no trouble hearing the intense sounds being produced.

A study of the Civil War literature shows that there were other battles in which acoustical events similar to those observed by Kean and Franklin occurred. More importantly, and in contrast to Gaines's Mill, there were battles in which the strange propagation of sound played a direct role in the outcome of the battle. The purpose of this book is to examine those battles in detail. That some battles can be affected by their own sounds is intrinsically interesting, and a compilation of such battles is yet another angle through which we can examine the war. But

I also hope to make some reasonable guesses as to what caused the unusual acoustics in each case. For each battle discussed, I have tried to give enough background information so that even those who are not Civil War buffs may be able to see the acoustics in the context of the battle and the battle in the context of the war.

Before one can fully appreciate the role of sound in the various Civil War battles, two preliminary topics must be understood. First, in chapter 2, we will look at the often-complicated ways in which sound moves through the air. What exactly caused Kean, Randolph and others to be unable to hear the battle of Gaines's Mill? Did it have something to do with the water content or temperature of the air, as Kean supposed in his letter? Did the dense forest around the battlefield play a part, as Franklin proposed? Are there other factors unknown to these gentlemen that may become important in such acoustic anomalies?

After laying the groundwork for understanding the propagation of sound on a battlefield, in chapter 3 we will examine the ways in which Civil War commanders used sound in formulating their pre-battle strategies and their command decisions during battle. Why would the lack of sound in a certain location on the field of combat be so catastrophic in some situations, but not in others? As we shall see, the Civil War occurred at a time when the size of armies had outgrown the ability of commanders to communicate with all the different parts of their command.

The remainder of the book deals with individual battles and the impact of sound propagation on their outcomes. By looking at terrain and period land cover, weather information, diaries, and regimental histories, as well as the wealth of primary and secondary sources surrounding each battle, we can piece together plausible reasons for why sounds of battle didn't reach commanders when one might expect those sounds to have been easily heard.

Chapter 2

Outdoor Sounds

What Is Sound?

The movement of sounds through the air outdoors is a complicated business even on the most placid day. Our air swirls in invisible whirlpools, streams up and down in reaction to temperature differences, and may vary considerably in moisture content from spot to spot. When the day is blustery or rainy it may seem a miracle that we hear anything at a distance. Let's start with the basics and try to understand what constitutes a sound, before tackling the problem of its motion through our atmosphere.

A sound is a wave and as such it constitutes a moving signal. Though sound can travel through solids, liquids, and gases, we will concentrate on the motion through air. The signal representing sound in air is an alteration in air pressure.[1] To visualize how such a signal can be created, consider a thin piece of metal (which we will call a reed), mounted vertically so that it can be made to vibrate (see fig. 2.1a). The reed, when struck, pushes air away from itself as it moves rapidly back and forth. The movement of the reed may be too fast to detect with the eye, but the motion can be revealed if you hold a suspended table tennis ball next to the metal so that it touches. The ball will be driven away with great force.

As the reed moves to the right (as shown in fig. 2.1b), molecules of nitrogen and oxygen (the main constituents of air) are pushed into their neighbors. This creates a localized region of higher than normal air density and pressure (called a *condensation* by physicists). This signal of increased pressure flies outward from the reed as other molecules

7

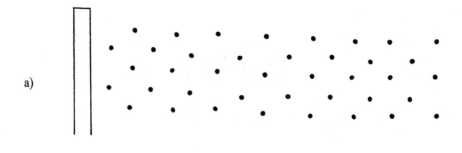

a)

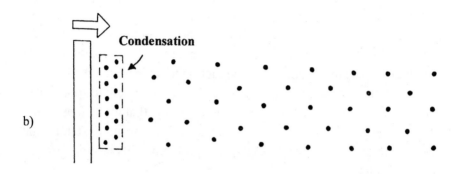

b)

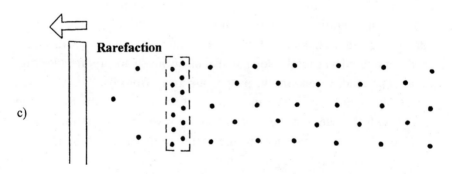

c)

Fig. 2.1. Condensations and Rarefactions

(*a*) A metal reed; the circles represent air molecules. (*b*) When the reed moves to the right, it compresses nearby air molecules into a high-pressure region called a condensation. (*c*) When the reed springs back to the left, it creates a low-pressure region called a rarefaction. Notice that the original condensation has moved to the right.

John M. Early

are, in turn, pushed into their neighbors. A one-dimensional analogy would be a line of people elbowing one another in turn as the signal passes down the line. The signal moves, while the people essentially remain in place. A two-dimensional analogy might be the infamous "Wave" that passes around sports stadiums. Although the condensations in the figure are drawn in two dimensions, the condensations (i.e., the signal of increased pressure) actually move away from the reed as something like an expanding sphere while the molecules that propagate the signal pretty much stay in place.

This expanding wave of increased pressure is followed immediately by a wave of decreased pressure as the reed moves back to the left. Molecules rush into the vacated space and this signal (called a *rarefaction*) follows right behind the condensation. The two signals thus created travel together as a pulse (see fig. 2.1c). This pulse transmits two pieces of information: the molecules have hit their outward neighbors and also that they have moved back toward their original locations (or, alternatively, that the reed has moved back and forth one time).

Frequency

If the reed moves repeatedly back and forth, a train of wave pulses is created (see fig. 2.2a, b). As this pattern of increasing and decreasing air pressure hits our eardrums, we associate a sensation we call *pitch* to the wave. The pitch of the wave corresponds directly to the *frequency* of the wave. The frequency of the wave is the number of times per second that a condensation hits our eardrums (or, alternatively, the number of times per second that the reed completes one back-and-forth cycle of motion).

For example, if the reed is made so that it moves back and forth about 260 times per second, the sound produced will be the pitch we associate with the note middle C on the piano. Its shape, size, and its constituent materials determine the particular frequency of such a reed. The lower the frequency, the lower the pitch and the higher the frequency, the higher the pitch. The common unit used by scientists to describe frequency is the *hertz* (abbreviated Hz) which means the same as "once per second." A healthy young person can detect sounds if the frequency is greater than about 20 Hz and less than about 20,000 Hz. Lower and higher frequencies are inaudible to humans but may be heard

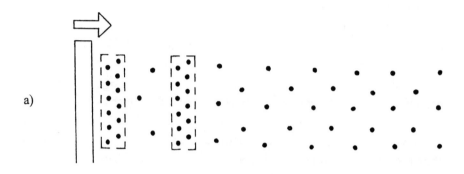

a)

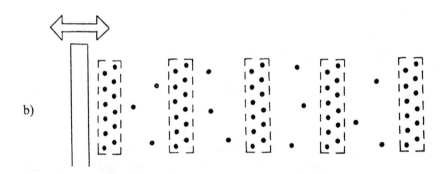

b)

Fig. 2.2. The Formation of a Sound Wave

(*a*) The reed moves back to the right and creates another condensation. (*b*) As the reed continues to move back and forth, a pattern of condensations and rarefactions moves away to the right—this is a sound wave.

John M. Early

by other creatures. This is the secret behind devices like dog whistles that create ultrasonic frequencies above 20,000 Hz. The pattern of pressure variations happens too rapidly for us to detect but has a great effect on a dog. The frequency range of hearing decreases with age and most middle-aged adults cannot hear sounds with frequencies higher than about 14,000 Hz.

More Complex Sounds

The sound created by a reed or tuning fork is called a pure tone, because it consists of one frequency.[2] Most sounds are more complicated and consist of a mixture of different frequencies. For example, when we strike the middle C key on the piano, the string inside will move in a complicated way that creates sounds not only of 260 Hz but also multiples of this frequency (i.e., 520 Hz, 780 Hz, 1040 Hz, etc.). The lowest frequency is called the *fundamental frequency,* or first *harmonic,* of the sound. Double this frequency (520 Hz in this case) is called the second harmonic and so on.

The various frequencies created when we strike the middle C key do not cause equal changes in air pressure. In other words, the intensity of the various harmonics is not the same. The relative mixture of the harmonics in a musical sound gives the sound a unique quality or timbre that we associate with that instrument. Thus, the same note sounds different when played on a piano and a guitar because of the relative mixture of harmonics created in each case.

Now let's begin to ponder the sounds of the Civil War. The sound of a cannon or rifle might be "music to the ears" if the weapon is on your side in a battle, but the sounds are obviously not musical in the usual sense. The sharp pulse of air pressure created when the explosion occurs in a gun barrel is certainly different from the pure tone of a reed or tuning fork and isn't much like the more complex tone of a musical instrument, either.

Fortunately, there is a way of understanding these cruder sounds. The French mathematician Jean Baptiste Fourier (1768–1830) discovered that any wave pulse, no matter what its shape, could be recreated by adding together pure tones of various intensities. The mathematics of doing so is relatively complicated, but the method is much like a cook adding the right amount of ingredients to a recipe. While the pure tone of a tuning fork requires but one "ingredient," the sharp pulse of a gunshot requires many different frequencies.

Still, even a complicated sound consisting of many frequencies tends to have one frequency that predominates. In the case of artillery, the predominant frequencies are in the range of 100 Hz, while for small arms the range is from 800 to 1,000 Hz.[3] These frequencies play an important part in the propagation of sound outdoors.

The Speed of Sound

The signals of alternating high and low pressure created by our reed travel through the air with a certain speed. This speed is about 1,100 feet per second or 12 miles per minute. This is certainly fast, but not so fast that we can't detect it. For example, while watching fireworks on the Fourth of July, one can easily sense the difference in speed between the light from the explosion (traveling at 186,000 miles per second) and the sound of the explosion.

Normally, this speed is the same for all frequencies of sound. It is lucky for us that this is so. Attending a concert would be a nightmare if the notes from the various instruments did not reach us simultaneously.

One important factor that can influence the speed of sound in air is the air temperature. In general, as the air becomes warmer and the constituent molecules have more energy, sounds travel through more rapidly. As air cools, sounds travel more slowly. At room temperature, the speed of sound in dry air is 1,131 feet per second. For every increase in temperature by one degree Fahrenheit, the speed of sound increases by about 1.1 feet per second.[4] Cooling temperatures decrease the speed by the same amount.

As we shall see shortly, this dependence of sound speed on temperature has important implications for the travel of sound outdoors. Since the temperature fluctuates from point to point within our atmosphere, different parts of a sound wave may move with different speeds. This can cause some interesting effects.

The Propagation of Outdoor Sounds

As one might expect, the movement of sound waves outdoors through our swirling atmosphere is complicated. We can, however, identify certain factors that will affect the movement of sound from place to place. Each of these factors will attenuate (affect the intensity of) the sound wave.

Geometrical Spreading

First, to eliminate the complications of the ground, trees, and so on, let's imagine that we are listening to a sound far out into space. Since sounds actually require some material to transport the signal and since space is virtually devoid of material, this is purely an imaginary exercise. For the purposes of the exercise, let's imagine that space is filled with air at about zero degrees Fahrenheit.

As soon as the source of the sound (imagine our reed again) has begun to vibrate, a spherical wave will expand away from it. After one second, the sphere will have a radius of about 1,100 feet. After two seconds, the sphere will have a radius of about 2,200 feet. After a minute, the radius will be about 12 miles.

Each condensation contains a certain amount of energy, transmitted to the air by the movement of the vibrating metal reed. As the circle gets bigger and bigger, this energy is spread over a larger and larger circumference and is therefore decreased in intensity. The sound pressure decreases by a factor of four when the radius grows by a factor of ten.[5]

One can see this effect by moving an object up and down in a still body of water. As the circular waves on the two-dimensional surface grow larger around, their height decreases as the energy intensity is diluted. The effect of this geometrical spreading of sound intensity can be explained in everyday language: As one gets farther from the source of a sound, the sound gets more and more faint. This is a common sense observation. Under certain circumstances, however, other effects may overpower this natural decrease in energy and make sounds louder at a greater distance from the source than at closer distances.

All frequencies of sound are affected by this decrease due to geometrical spreading in the same way. As described later in this chapter, however, the human ear is not equally sensitive to all frequencies. As the sounds decrease in intensity with distance, we lose our ability to hear the very low- and very high-frequency sounds much sooner than notes of a moderate frequency. All other factors being equal, one would hear a rifle at a greater distance than a cannon due to this effect.

Atmospheric Absorption

As a sound wave makes its way through the atmosphere, the molecules in the air may rob the wave of some of its energy. At audible frequencies, the main source of this energy loss is due to the energy of the sound wave being converted into internal vibrations of oxygen and nitrogen molecules. One can imagine these N_2 and O_2 molecules as microscopic dumbbell shapes, with two oxygen atoms (in the O_2 molecule) attached by a springlike bond. As the sound wave passes, the atoms begin to oscillate back and forth along the line of the bond. The energy required for this motion has been absorbed from the sound wave.

Water vapor in the air can have a catalytic effect on this molecular absorption, especially if the air temperature is warm.[6] In the range of frequencies produced by Civil War weapons, the atmospheric absorption comes mainly from the nitrogen molecules.

The Effect of the Ground

Now imagine that we bring our metal reed to earth. This gives rise to a number of new complications in understanding the propagation of the sound to our ears. First, part of our expanding sphere of sound energy will immediately hit the ground. In general, some of this sound energy will be reflected off the ground and some will be absorbed.

The amount of sound absorbed by the ground is obviously determined by the nature of the surface. As surfaces get softer, they tend to absorb more of the sound energy and to do so at lower and lower frequencies. For example, newly fallen snow absorbs more sound than a sandy surface. The sandy surface absorbs more than a grass-covered surface, which in turn absorbs quite a bit more than asphalt. The frequency of maximum absorption is around 125 Hz for snow and over 2,000 Hz for asphalt.[7]

The main surface of concern for analyzing Civil War battles is grass. Grass tends to absorb a maximum amount of sound energy at frequencies around 300 to 400 Hz. This is a bit above the main frequencies of artillery and a bit below the main frequencies of small arms. The effect is not symmetric around this minimum, however, and grass-covered surfaces will absorb small arms fire sounds much more effectively than the low frequencies of artillery.

Grass cover can sometimes actually make the sounds of artillery louder than otherwise. This effect can be attributed to a phenomenon known as *interference*. Waves, not being made of matter, can do something that physical objects cannot: two waves can be in the same place at the same time. When this occurs, the piece of matter through which the waves are moving must respond to two signals at once. For example, suppose a molecule in the air is hit by a condensation (i.e., the message to "move to the right") from one wave as it is simultaneously hit by a rarefaction (i.e., the message to "move to the left") by a second wave. If the intensities of the waves are equal, the molecule will do nothing. The signals from the waves have cancelled each other out, a phenomenon known as *destructive interference.*

If the molecule is hit by two rarefactions (or two condensations) of equal intensity, it will move more than if hit by one wave alone. This effect is known as *constructive interference.* In the case of a low-frequency sound (like that from artillery) on a grass-covered surface, the wave that reflects off the ground can actually join back with a wave heading directly toward the listener to make the sound louder than normal. Acousticians call this *negative attenuation.*

When the land is not open, but covered with trees, this negative attenuation may not be so important. The root structure of the trees will make the ground more porous and will increase the absorption of low frequencies so that the reflected waves are greatly decreased in intensity. This makes the reflected wave much less effective in causing negative attenuation.

The Effect of Trees and Foliage

The trees themselves will also have an effect on the sound waves. The trunks, the branches, and foliage all come into play. All will tend to decrease the intensity of the sound wave by absorbing the wave or by redirecting the wave from its original path. The degree to which the sounds are affected is again determined by the frequency. In higher frequencies, the condensations are closer together than for a lower frequency. Another way of saying this is that higher frequencies have a shorter *wavelength.*

The interaction between the sound and the trees becomes more pronounced as the wavelength and the particular part of the tree become more similar in size. The sounds of small arms fire have a wavelength (i.e., distance between successive condensations) of about one foot while the sounds of artillery have a wavelength more on the order of 10 feet. This means that in most cases trees and foliage attenuate the sounds of small arms fire much more heavily than they attenuate the sounds of artillery.

To cause a significant decrease in sound intensity, the foliage must be very dense, have large leaves (to better match the wavelength of the sounds) and must have significant depth between the sound source and the listener. If one can see for a considerable distance through the foliage, the effect will be minimal.[8]

Barriers and Obstructions

Any solid object that blocks the line of sight between the sound source and the listener has the potential for decreasing sound intensity. This could be a wall, a house, or a mountain. The effect has been shown to be most pronounced when either the source or listener is close to the barrier.[9] The effect is also usually more important for high frequencies. The lower frequencies with their larger wavelengths tend to spread around the edges of the barriers unless the barrier is very large.

Refraction

We now come to a most important phenomenon for understanding the propagation of outdoor sounds. Under certain conditions, waves can change direction, or *refract*. Such an effect might obviously have a large influence on the ability of a potential listener to hear a sound.

First, we need to think of our expanding sphere of sound a bit differently. Imagine that someone dropped an enormous object in the middle of the Atlantic Ocean. By the time the wave from this event reached an observer on the East Coast of the United States, the part this observer sees will appear to be a straight line. This is because the original circle has expanded to such great size that it is hard to see its curvature in any particular section encountered (see fig. 2.3). In a somewhat similar way, when one walks across the surface of the earth it appears flat because the sphere upon which one walks is so large.

Looking at one of these straight parts of a larger spherical wave does not change the nature of the signal. The frequency, wavelength, and so on will be the same as for the larger wave. These flat sections of wave are called *plane waves*, and they make understanding refraction much easier.

Now, imagine a line of people marching hand-in-hand (see fig. 2.4a) across a muddy area. As they come to a paved area (see fig. 2.4b), the people entering the paved area begin to move faster. The net effect of this (see fig. 2.4c) is that the entire line of people will have changed direction by the time they are all on the paved area. In similar fashion, if a plane wave enters a region in which its speed changes, it can change direction (or refract).

The Refractive Effect of Temperature

As discussed earlier in this chapter, air temperature can affect the speed of sound waves. The air around us is never at one uniform temperature. Temperatures vary from point to point and also from second to second at any given point. Temperature fluctuations of 10 to 20 degrees Fahrenheit for a few seconds are common. This means that our nice flat plane wave will quickly become distorted as different parts of the wave speed up or slow down. A similar refractive effect of air temperature on light waves produces the twinkling of stars. This distortion due to nonhomogeneous air temperatures is usually not so severe that it prevents sounds from being recognized, but will become more severe at greater distance from the source as the sound passes through more air.

A more important temperature effect for our discussion stems from the natural stratification of temperatures in our atmosphere. In the lower atmosphere, temperatures normally decrease as one increases altitude. This lower atmosphere, called the troposphere, rises to a height of between 6 and 12 miles. At an altitude of 36,000 feet (between 6 and 7 miles), the speed of sound will have dropped from its sea level value of 760 miles per hour to only 660 miles per hour due to this temperature difference.[10]

Above this layer is another layer of air called the stratosphere that rises for another 30 miles. The air in the stratosphere is less dense than that in the troposphere. In the stratosphere, temperatures can

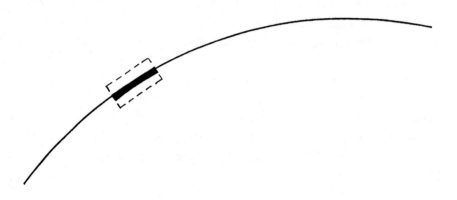

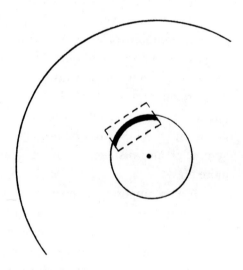

Fig. 2.3. A Plane Wave

As a wave gets farther from its source, any section encountered is more like a plane than a sphere.

John M. Early

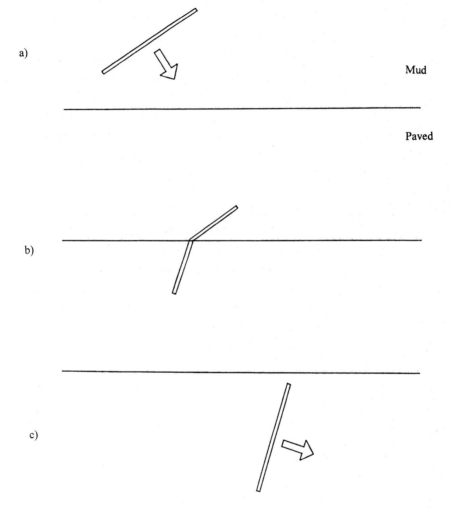

a)

Mud

Paved

b)

c)

Fig. 2.4. A Refraction Analogy

(*a*) The line represents a row of people walking together through mud with arms linked. (*b*) Now the people on the paved area are walking faster than those still in the mud. (*c*) By the time the entire row of people has entered the paved area, the direction of the row has changed. A similar effect causes waves to refract when they enter a region in which wave speed changes.

John M. Early

actually increase with increasing altitude due to the absorption of solar radiation by ozone molecules.

Concentrating on the troposphere for now, we can see the normal refractive effect of temperature in figure 2.5a. The lower part of our plane wave is traveling in warmer (i.e., faster) air near the ground and as a result the entire wave is refracted upwards. This makes one less likely to hear the sound at ground level the farther one is from the source.

A notable experiment in the 1800s by Osborne Reynolds demonstrated that this effect can be quite pronounced even at low altitudes. Reynolds placed a ringing bell on a one-foot high pedestal and then crawled away from it. At a distance of about 20 yards, Reynolds could no longer hear the bell at ground level. When he raised his head a bit, the sound could again be heard. He continued to crawl and found that at 70 yards, he could hear the bell only by standing.[11]

Sometimes, however, the lower atmosphere exhibits a temperature profile of exactly the opposite character. During a temperature inversion, the air becomes warmer as one moves away from the ground. Temperature inversions are common at night as the ground radiates away its stored heat. They can also occur in the morning following a clear cold night (fog is often a good indicator that an inversion is present) and during widespread rainstorms.

In figure 2.5b, we can see the effect of a temperature inversion. Sound waves that would normally be lost into space can be refracted back down to earth. This means that a person far from the source of sound might hear the sound extraordinarily well. In general, this means that sounds are heard better than normal during a temperature inversion.[12]

The Refractive Effect of Wind Shear

Similar refractive effects can be caused by wind, or more exactly, by what is called *wind shear*. Figure 2.6 shows a typical profile of wind speeds, with the arrows representing the relative speed of the wind at different heights. As altitude increases, wind speeds generally increase also as frictional effects from the ground and structures become less important. This variation in wind speed with height is wind shear.

In figure 2.6 we see the effect of wind shear on sound propagation. For plane waves heading into the wind, the lower part of the wave

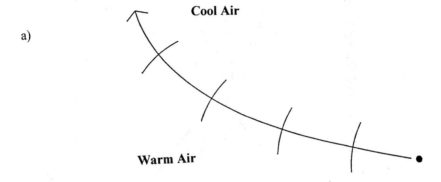

a)

Cool Air

Warm Air

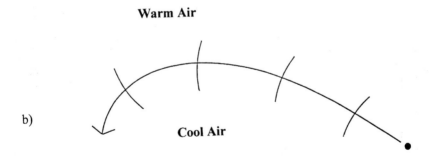

Warm Air

b)

Cool Air

Fig. 2.5. Temperature-Induced Refraction

(*a*) Normally, temperatures are lower higher up and sounds refract upward. (*b*) In a temperature inversion, sounds can refract back to earth.

John M. Early

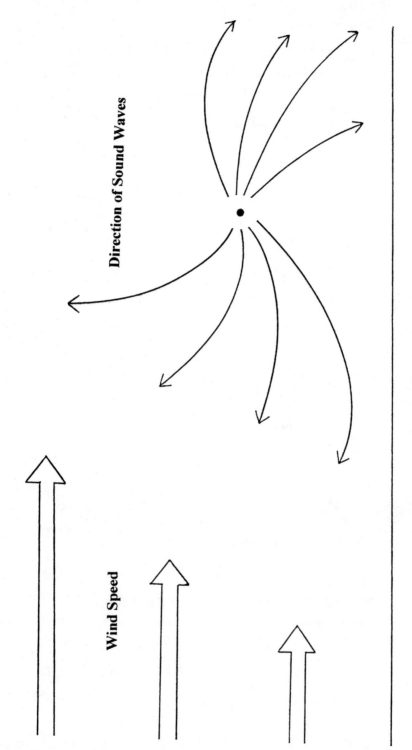

Fig. 2.6. The Effects of Wind Shear

Sounds headed into the wind refract upward; sounds headed downwind refract downward.

John M. Early

encounters slower winds than does the upper part. As the lower part of the wave is thus less impeded by the wind, the entire wave front will swing around or refract upwards. The opposite situation occurs down-wind from the source as the high altitude winds now help refract the wave down towards the ground. As a result of wind shear, sounds are typically heard better downwind from the source than upwind. This is a common sense observation, but remember that the lack of audibility upwind is not due to the sound being "blown" back to the source as one might first think. The sound does travel in the upwind direction, but is refracted over the listener's head.

An interesting example of what was apparently wind-induced re-fraction in the Civil War occurred on March 8, 1862, when the ironclad CSS *Virginia* (formerly the USS *Merrimack*) attacked the Union fleet at Hampton Roads. Confederate Brigadier R. E. Colston, in charge of a brigade on the south side of the James River, watched the battle and later wrote an account. In his description of the fight, he notes some unusual acoustics:

> A curious incident must be noted here. Great numbers of people from the neighborhood of Ragged Island, as well as sol-diers from the nearest posts, had rushed to the shore to behold the spectacle. The cannonade was visibly raging with redoubled in-tensity; but, to our amazement, not a sound was heard by us from the commencement of the battle. A strong March wind was blow-ing direct from us toward Newport News. We could see every flash of the guns and the clouds of white smoke, but not a single report was audible.[13]

Acoustic Shadows and Unusual Audibility at Long Range

Notice in both figures 2.5 and 2.6 (for observers upwind from the source) that potential observers are often left in what is sometimes called an *acoustic shadow* zone. If the wind shear or temperature gra-dient is particularly strong, an observer may be fairly close to the source (even within sight of it) and yet be unable to hear it. Hence, the obser-vations of Randolph and Kean in chapter 1 are not implausible.

A small amount of the original sound wave energy can still enter the shadow zone by creeping along the ground. This creeping wave quickly drops off with distance from the source, though, and more strongly for higher frequencies than for low. Thus, the sounds of musketry are less likely to creep into the shadow than are those of artillery.

As we will see when looking at several Civil War battles, a commander who inadvertently placed himself upwind from the scene of the fighting could find himself in an acoustic shadow. Equally interesting (though of less importance to historians) is the fate of those sounds that passed over the head of our commander. It turns out that while these sounds typically dissipate into the upper atmosphere, under certain conditions they can be brought back to earth. This can occur if the sound wave encounters a strong temperature inversion or wind shear in the upper atmosphere (even at the level of the stratosphere if the sound is strong).

Recall from our discussion of temperature-induced refraction that temperatures in the stratosphere can actually be higher than that of the lower air. Temperatures at 30 miles above the earth may be as high as 120 degrees Fahrenheit.[14] As the upper part of our plane wave enters such a region, it will speed up and turn the entire wave back towards the earth. It will, however, lose some of its strength due to the decreased density of air at that height. (This lack of oxygen and pressure would also make this region quite inhospitable to humans without proper equipment.)

This effect is most pronounced when there is strong upward refraction close to the source and strong downward refraction aloft. The net result is that someone far from the source may be able to hear it better than someone closeby. Stranger still, if the downward refracted wave reflects off the ground with sufficient intensity it can rise again and repeat the cycle. This can lead to a "bull's-eye" pattern of rings of audibility and inaudibility around the source (see fig. 2.7). These rings can be many miles in width.

The winds most responsible for this sort of refraction occur above 6 miles. These winds reverse direction seasonally at temperate latitudes, and this causes long-range propagation of sound to be better from east to west in the summer and from west to east in the winter. The battles of World War I were heard much more clearly in England during the summer and in Germany during the winter. Since most Civil War fighting occurred during the warmer months, most cases of long-range audibility noted then were to the west of the battle.

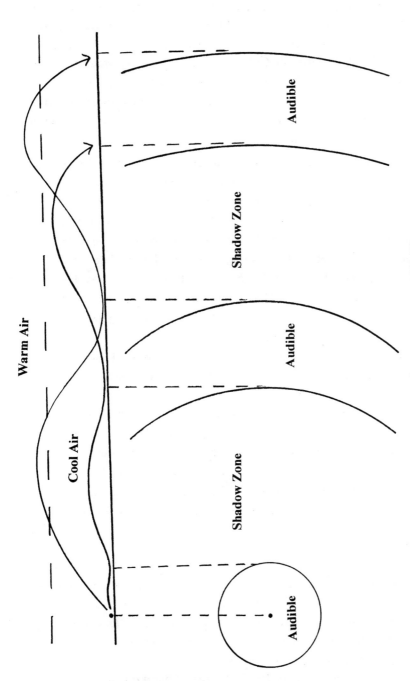

Fig. 2.7. Long-Range Audibility

Temperature inversions (or wind shear) can refract sounds back to earth, only to be reflected back up. Overhead view shows the resulting pattern of regions of audibility and acoustic shadow zones

John M. Early

As shown in figure 2.7, these cases of long-range audibility often go hand-in-hand with strong upward refraction and acoustic shadows near the source. One example was noted in chapter 1. Although observers close to the battle of Gaines's Mill apparently watched in silence, more than one report exists of the sounds of the fighting being carried far to the western part of Virginia. Another example occurred during the Union bombardment of Port Royal, South Carolina. A Union soldier wrote after the war:

> At the bombardment of the Confederate works at Port Royal, South Carolina, in November 1861, the transport my regiment was on lay near enough inshore to give us a fine view of the whole battle; but only in some temporary lull of the wind could we hear the faintest sound of firing. The day was a pleasant one, and the wind did not appear to be unusually strong; but I noticed then and afterward that a breeze on the coast down that way was very different from the erratic gusts and flaws that I had been used to in the New England States, the whole atmosphere seeming to move in a body, giving sound no chance to travel against it, but carrying it immense distances to the leeward. People living in St. Augustine, Florida, told me afterward that the Port Royal cannonade was heard at that place, 150 miles from where the fighting took place. A portion of the siege-batteries at Morris Island, South Carolina, were not more than two miles from our camp, but at times the firing from them and the enemy's replies could only be heard very faintly even at that short distance, while at others, when the wind blew from the opposite direction, the sounds were as sharp and distinct as if the battle were taking place within a few rods of us.[15]

Hearing

A few words about hearing are in order at this point in our discussion. Though the main point of the book is to examine the propagation of sound through the air, we would be remiss if we failed to consider how a listener receives these sounds. The structure of the ear is fairly complex, but the sensation of hearing is created when the sound wave transmits its pressure variations to the eardrum.

One interesting aspect of hearing is that it has a threshold. In other words, if the sound wave carries less than a certain amount of energy we hear nothing. There may be pressure variations being transmitted around us, but we will still hear nothing if they are of insufficient strength. This same sort of threshold behavior holds for our other senses as well.

What is the smallest amount of energy one can detect with the eardrums? This depends to a great deal on the frequency of the sound. The human ear is much more sensitive to sounds in the range from 1,000 Hz to 5,000 Hz than to sounds with either greater or lower frequency. A 500 Hz sound must be made much more intense than a 1,000 Hz sound for us to perceive them as being equally loud. Below about 20 Hz or above approximately 20,000 Hz, we are unable to pick up the sound no matter what the intensity.

For the purposes of our study, this means that we would expect soldiers to be much more responsive to the sounds of musketry (at roughly 800–1,000 Hz) than to that of artillery (at roughly 100 Hz).

One other aspect of hearing pertinent to the current study is that our ability to hear deteriorates with age, as the mechanism of the ear becomes less supple. We can also expect that career military men have been exposed to a greater than average number of explosive sounds, which will also tend to make hearing deteriorate. This may help to explain at least one occasion we will examine in the Civil War in which younger staff officers could not convince a general that the sounds of battle were audible.

The History of Atmospheric Acoustics

How well did those affected by acoustic shadows in the Civil War understand the nature of the phenomenon? It is useful to have some perspective on where the war fits into the history of the study of atmospheric acoustics.

The earliest recorded observation of abnormal audibility and acoustic shadow zones seems to have been made by the English diarist Samuel Pepys in June 1666. According to Pepys, the sounds of a naval engagement between the British and Dutch fleets were heard clearly at some spots in England but not at others. Pepys also spoke to the captain of a yacht that had been positioned between the battle and the English coast. The captain said he had seen the fleets and had run from them, "…but from that hour to this hath not heard one gun…." Pepys adds that the curious incident "makes room for a great dispute in philosophy how we should hear it and they not, the same wind that brought it to us being the same that should bring it to them; but it is so!"[16]

The acoustician Cicely Botley has noted that there may be another, even earlier case of unusual audibility. It is stated that the sound of the preliminary bombardment by the Ottoman Turks before their attack on Rhodes in May 1480 was heard 100 miles away.[17]

The scientific study of atmospheric acoustics apparently began in 1704 when William Derham reported to the Royal Society on the effects of wind, barometric pressure, temperature, and humidity on sound propagation.[18] Derham and an Italian acquaintance named Averrani also showed that sound propagation did not differ in the two countries.[19]

Between these earliest beginnings in the field and the Civil War, very little progress appears to have been made. A thorough investigation of outdoor sound propagation began in 1873 when John Tyndall (the British scientist mentioned as the recipient of Kean's letter in chapter 1) began a systematic series of experiments of sound propagation in the Straits of Dover. The impetus for his investigation was the problem of fog for ships. Since light was quickly absorbed in the fog, sound was naturally used as a signal that shore was near. All sorts of bells, horns, whistles, sirens, and even guns were tried with varying success. It was obvious that unusual effects often made the warning sounds inaudible to those on the ships.

An 1863 letter by an Irish scientist to the British Board of Trade clearly shows the state of knowledge at the time of the Civil War:

> Sound is the only means really effective; but about it testimonies are conflicting, and there is scarcely one fact relating to its use as a signal which can be considered as established. Even the most important of all, the distance at which it ceases to be heard, is undecided.
>
> Up to the present time all signal-sounds have been made in the air, though this medium has grave disadvantages: its own currents interfere with the sound-waves, so that a gun or bell which is heard several miles down the wind is inaudible more than a few furlongs up it.[20]

Using all sorts of sound sources, including a gigantic foghorn lent to him by the U.S. Lighthouse Board (see fig. 2.8), Tyndall and his assistants made careful observations of sound propagation under various weather conditions. The sound sources were located on the Dover shore, while Tyndall stationed himself on a boat in the Straits of Dover.

Tyndall found a bewildering range of inconsistencies in his results. Sometimes the sounds could be heard farther against the wind, sometimes farther with the wind. At times the high-frequency whistles were heard better than the lower-frequency guns and sometimes the reverse was true. Occasionally, propagation was better in bad weather than in good weather, the reverse of what Derham propounded 170 years previous.

An excerpt from his journal reveals the sorts of observations Tyndall was able to make:

> On the morning of October 8th, at 7.45 A.M., a thunderstorm accompanied by heavy rain broke over Dover. But the clouds subsequently cleared away, and the sun shone strongly on the sea. For a time the optical clearness of the atmosphere was extraordinary, but it was acoustically opaque. At 2.30 P.M. a densely-black scowl again overspread the heavens to the W.S.W. The distance being 6 miles, and all hushed on board, the horn was heard very feebly, the siren more distinctly, while the howitzer was better than either, though not much superior to the siren.
>
> A squall approached us from the west. In the Alps or elsewhere I have rarely seen the heavens blacker. Vast cumuli floated to the N.E. and S.E.; vast streamers of rain descended in the W.N.W.; huge scrolls of cloud hung in the N.; but spaces of blue were to be seen to the N.N.E.
>
> At 7 miles' distance the siren and horn were both feeble, while the gun sent us a very faint report. A dense shower now developed the Foreland.
>
> The rain at length reached us, falling heavily all the way between us and the Foreland; but the sound, instead of being deadened, rose perceptibly in power. Hail was now added to the rain, and the shower reached a tropical violence, the hailstones floating thickly on the flooded deck. In the midst of this furious squall both the horns and the siren were distinctly heard; and as the shower

Fig. 2.8. John Tyndall's Foghorn

Tyndall, *Sound*

lightened, thus lessening the local pattering, the sounds so rose in power that we heard them at a distance of 7^1/$_2$ miles distinctly louder than they had been heard through the rainless atmosphere at 5 miles.[21]

Tyndall found that on a hazy day, the sounds might be heard more than 12 miles from shore while on a calm and clear day the range might be as little as 4 miles. Sometimes the range would change between these two extremes on a single day with little perceptible change in the weather. Tyndall was able to experience the acoustic shadow phenomenon, and noted many occasions when the sound was completely inaudible close to the sound sources, only to become audible again much farther from shore.

Tyndall eventually concluded that the air contained "acoustic clouds," invisible entities capable of strongly reflecting sound in various directions. Though he was incorrect in attributing the acoustic anomalies mainly to reflection instead of refraction, he was correct in concluding that the source of unusual sound propagation was the inhomogeneous nature of the air.

At about the same time that Tyndall was working in England, the eclectic American scientist Joseph Henry was also looking into the problem. His studies off the coast of Rhode Island led him to conclude that Tyndall was wrong in his "acoustic cloud" hypothesis. Henry's conclusion was that much of the unusual sound propagation observations could be attributed to reflection off the surface waves of the water. This was also off the mark.

Despite the lack of scientific knowledge regarding acoustic anomalies, their existence in the Civil War was common knowledge by the end of the 19th century. This probably came in part from widespread dissemination of Kean's letter to Tyndall after the publication of Tyndall's book. The observations by Evander M. Law in chapter 1 may have come from an independent eyewitness, but they have the ring of hearsay, something like the "urban legends" of modern times. The American writer Ambrose Bierce wrote a short piece in the late 1800s (possibly from firsthand experience, as he fought in the war) in which an acoustic anomaly occurs. An excerpt shows how Kean's observations had crept into the public domain:

A hundred yards away was a straight road, showing white in the moonlight. Endeavoring to orient himself, as a surveyor or navigator might say, the man moved his eyes slowly along its visible length and at a distance of a quarter-mile to the south of his station saw, dim and gray in the haze, a group of horsemen riding to the north. Behind them were men afoot, marching in column, with dimly gleaming rifles aslant above their shoulders. They moved slowly and in silence. Another group of horsemen, another regiment of infantry, another and another—all in unceasing motion toward the man's point of view, past it, and beyond. A battery of artillery followed, the cannoneers riding with folded arms on limber and caisson. And still the interminable procession came out of the obscurity to the south and passed into obscurity to north, with never a sound of voice, nor hoof, nor wheel.

The man could not rightly understand: he thought himself deaf; said so, and heard his own voice, although it had an unfamiliar quality that almost alarmed him; it disappointed the ear's expectancy in the matter of *timbre* and resonance. But he was not deaf, and that for the moment sufficed.

Then he remembered that there are natural phenomena to which some one has given the name 'acoustic shadows.' If you stand in an acoustic shadow there is one direction from which you will hear nothing. At the battle of Gaines's Mill, one of the fiercest conflicts of the Civil War, with a hundred guns in play, spectators a mile and a half away on the opposite side of the Chickahominy valley heard nothing of what they clearly saw.[22]

It is a little strange that the man in Bierce's story, which seems to take place during the Civil War, would remember something that was not common knowledge at the time. However, the story does serve as an indication that many people knew that acoustic shadows had existed during the war. Later in the story Bierce also alludes to the unusual acoustics at Port Royal, South Carolina, and at Five Forks, Virginia.

It was not until the 20th century that scientists arrived at a deeper understanding of atmospheric acoustics. Balloon measurements led to the discovery of the stratosphere, the layer of calm air above our turbulent lower atmosphere, in 1902.[23] In the previous year, on the occasion of Queen Victoria's funeral, the sound from a battery of guns fired in London was heard in Scotland but not in a wide range in between.[24]

In 1910, a Dutch scientist made the first detailed measurements of the rings of audibility and inaudibility around an explosion. These types of measurements were given a great deal of attention during and following World War I. As noted earlier in this chapter, many observers had noted that the battles in France were heard better in England during that summer and in Germany during the winter. Many had also noted the sporadic nature of the acoustics around the battles.

During the bombardment of Antwerp in 1914, collected observations confirmed that within a 60-mile radius of the city the explosions were heard at most locations. Between 60 and 90 miles from Antwerp there were no reports of the sound being audible. Farther than 90 miles to the northeast, however, many observers in Holland and Germany reported hearing the sounds.[25]

In 1916, it was hypothesized that such zones of silence could be understood if there existed a temperature inversion at great height.[26] This upper level inversion was first deduced in 1923 by the study of meteor trails. A year later, Erwin Schrödinger (who became famous later for his role in the development of quantum mechanics) proposed that low-frequency sounds would be absorbed less in the atmosphere and would therefore be refracted back to earth more strongly than would high-frequency sounds.

There was great curiosity about the phenomenon after the war. Just after the war, large quantities of explosives were detonated throughout Germany, and the concentric rings of audibility and inaudibility were noted.[27] In 1927, cannons were fired at the Shoeburyness range near the mouth of the Thames and the sounds of the explosion broadcast by radio.[28] The time interval between the essentially instantaneous radio sound and the arrival of the actual sound was reported by observers throughout England. The sound arrived at Birmingham (130 miles from the guns) after a delay of 705 seconds. The time required for direct transmission was calculated at 610 seconds, meaning that the sound received had passed through the upper atmosphere. This not only meant that the sound had passed over a longer pathway than the direct route, but had spent a good portion of its transit time in cooler air with a lower velocity.

Rings of audibility and inaudibility were also observed, sometimes over great distances, with the atomic bomb tests in the western United States during the 1950s. In 1951, sounds from a bomb test struck Las Vegas, about 65 miles from the site of the blast. Investigation showed that the sound waves had refracted and then reflected with "focal points" every 11 miles. In other words, the sound wave had hit and bounced off the desert surface at 11 miles, 22 miles, 33 miles, 44 miles, 55 miles, and 66 miles from the blast. The sixth "hop" brought it into Las Vegas, where it shattered numerous windows.

The test site was moved farther away (to a distance of about 80 miles from Las Vegas), but on at least one occasion Las Vegas was hit again. This time it was by two waves, one with a focal length, or "hopping distance," of $6\frac{2}{3}$ miles (which hit Las Vegas on the twelfth hop) and the other 40 miles (which hit Las Vegas on the second hop).[29]

On many occasions, the sound waves from these atomic blasts were heard at long distances. Indeed, the sounds were heard more often at St. George and Cedar City, Utah, 130 and 150 miles from the test site in Nevada, than at Las Vegas. Sound waves, reflected three times from the desert with a focal length of more than 200 miles, were heard in Albuquerque, New Mexico, 640 miles from the test site and 48 minutes after the actual explosion.

Rings of audibility in the lower atmosphere rarely give focal points lying farther than 30 to 40 miles apart.[30] Focal lengths greater than this must be caused by temperature inversions higher up. There are two possible regions for this sort of inversion. One is the ozonosphere, at altitudes of roughly 10 to 30 miles, and the other is the "E-layer" of the ionosphere, at a height of about 60 miles. Both of these regions can bend sound waves back to earth, with focal lengths from 60 miles to around 200 miles. The air in the ionosphere is so rarified, however, that waves refracted from that height are likely to have lost most of their original intensity.

Summary

The propagation of sound through the atmosphere is an extremely complex topic and is still being studied. We can, however, compress the various mechanisms into several possible categories. If a person is outside, near a loud source, and does not hear it, the acoustic shadow is likely to stem from some combination of these factors:

- ✗ Absorption by foliage or a large land mass
- ✗ Upward refraction due to temperature differences in the air
- ✗ Upward refraction due to wind shear

We can also add the possible complication of diminished hearing in older, career military men.

Before looking at some individual battles in which acoustic shadows played a role, chapter 3 will offer a brief review of the ways in which information was transferred during the Civil War. This will help us to see why sound could play such an important role in command decisions.

Chapter 3

Tactical Communications in the Civil War

To understand why sound propagation could play an important role in a Civil War battle, it is helpful to understand the part played by sound in command decisions and communications during that time. Sight is naturally the most reliable of a general's senses when accumulating information, but a direct view of all parts of a Civil War battle was not always possible. The battlefronts often stretched for miles, over wooded and hilly terrain, and accommodated thousands of soldiers. So, how was a general of that time to obtain information about the disposition of his forces and those of the enemy? When a command decision was made, how was the information to be transmitted to all parts of the army?

Today, we take real-time communications for granted. Signals exist as electromagnetic waves or as electrical currents and travel at speeds near that of light in vacuum. With an upper velocity of 186,000 miles per second, our communications are all but instantaneous. A modern commander may be able to get almost instantaneous feedback about the progress of a battle through computer links to satellites and reconnaissance planes. He will also have near-instantaneous communication with subordinate commanders on the field of battle.

Communication techniques during the Civil War were primitive by comparison. There were some near-instantaneous techniques available on a limited basis, and these will be described shortly. For the most part, though, information traveled at a pace that was excruciatingly slow by today's standards.

As mentioned above, direct vision was and is the best source of feedback regarding the course of a battle. Without modern communication links, this meant that a Civil War officer would often have to place himself in a position of some danger in order to see as much as possible. This would be an unthinkable situation today, when commanders are normally far behind the front lines. The obvious downside for Civil War officers was the threat of being wounded or killed, something that happened with regularity throughout the war.

An essential piece of equipment for an officer was some means of enhancing his natural vision, usually a pair of binoculars or a telescope. It also helped his cause that (assuming the general officer was middle-aged or older) he would be surrounded by younger aides, with vision probably better than his. Through the use of various optical instruments, a general might extend his view of the battlefield to some miles depending on the terrain and type of land cover.

A veteran eye could deduce vital information from a variety of visual signals. The sight of a cloud of dust was often used to determine the movement of the enemy, and its speed to differentiate infantry from cavalry. The Union surprise attack at First Manassas was given away when Confederate signal officer Captain Edward P. Alexander saw something unexpected in the distance:

> While watching the flag of this station with a good glass, when I had been there about a half-hour, the sun being low in the east behind me, my eye was caught by a glitter in the narrow band of green. I recognized it at once as the reflection of the morning sun from a brass field-piece. Closer scrutiny soon revealed the glittering of bayonets and musket barrels.
>
> It was about 8.45 A.M., and I had discovered McDowell's turning column, the head of which, at this hour, was just arriving at Sudley, eight miles away.[1]

Alexander immediately signaled to the Confederate advance units: "Look out for your left; you are turned." He did this by moving a series of flags in a sequence of coded motions known as semaphore, or wigwag. The system was developed in the late 1850s by Albert J. Myer based on his observation of the signaling techniques of the Plains Indians (Alexander had been his assistant in the field tests of the system). A version of the system could be used at night with torches instead of flags. A similar sort of visual signal system, though less complex, was sometimes used between shore and naval vessels. Here the signaling was accomplished by use of calcium lights, which mixed calcium carbide (from limestone) with water to make brightly burning acetylene.

There were two obvious problems with the flag system, though it continued to be used through the war. First, the sender and receiver needed to be in direct visual contact. Thus, signal stations were often placed on prominent heights. Second, and more importantly, the information thus transmitted was as available to the enemy as to the intended receiver.

Alexander also transmitted his information about the Union movement to commanding General Joseph E. Johnston by means of a courier on horseback. By far the most popular means of transferring information on the Civil War battlefield, a retinue of such couriers accompanied most commanders. A commander would send orders through couriers (more than one courier would often carry the same information along different routes for purposes of redundancy) and would obtain information by the same means. An example of the means by which a group of couriers could be used is shown in the following account from the First Manassas. Here, Confederate Generals Johnston and P.G.T. Beauregard tried to understand the increasingly confusing events unfolding on that hot July day in 1861:

> When the sudden increase of fire broke out, which marked the arrival on the field of Bee and Bartow, Johnston seemed so restless that Beauregard was moved to despatch a staff-officer, Maj. Stevens, with a half-dozen couriers, under orders to ride rapidly, learn the situation, and send back a messenger every ten minutes.[2]

Though couriers were usually dependable and remained popular as a means of transmitting information throughout the war, there were some drawbacks. First was the speed with which the intelligence could be moved from one spot to another. Even at breakneck speed, a courier would lose several minutes, perhaps crucial minutes, getting from one end of a battlefield to the other. Second, there remained a very good possibility that the courier would not make it to the intended destination. He might become lost in the chaos of the battlefield, or he might be killed, captured, or wounded. Or the courier might find (as we will see at Iuka) that it is physically impossible to cross the terrain between the two segments of his army in a reasonable amount of time.

An obvious improvement in communication could be made by using a technology that was young, but well developed, at the time of the war. This was the telegraph, the first communication technique that could deliver information essentially instantaneously between two parties not in line of sight with each other. The telegraph had been made practical in the 1830s and had quickly spread across the United States and across the world. By the time of the war, telegraph lines connected most of the larger cities in New England and the Midwest. Two main lines in the South (one running from Washington to New Orleans and the other connecting Louisville to New Orleans) provided access to most of the major cities there also.

This network of telegraph lines was in constant use during the war and often played a role in strategic planning. For example, a telegram from Confederate President Jefferson Davis in Richmond to Joseph Johnston in Winchester prompted that general to move his forces quickly to the aid of Beauregard at Manassas. Though useful, these established lines were of little use on the battlefield. A tactical and mobile telegraph system would be of far greater value.

Union forces used such a system for part of the war and saw some success with it at Fredericksburg in December 1863. There, it allowed Union commanders to monitor events on that smoky and foggy battlefield. The system performed poorly at Chancellorsville in May of 1863, however, and subsequently it saw limited action for the rest of the war. The Union field telegraph "trains" consisted of battery wagons and huge reels of telegraph wire that were placed on the backs of mules so that the wire could be fed across the battlefield. The Confederates strung a few temporary telegraph lines for observation purposes, but made no use of the telegraph in the field due to limited resources.

One interesting usage of the telegraph was in conjunction with another set of "eyes" for several Civil War commanders: observation balloons. Balloonists on both sides used aerial observation to some extent, but this was practical in a tactical situation only if the balloons could be inflated near the battlefield. The Confederates, who had to rely on the coal gas (normally used for street lighting) in the larger cities to inflate their balloons, could not often do this. This worked when the battles happened to occur near a city (as in the Seven Days' battles

Fig. 3.1. *The Dispatch Bearer*

From the painting by Gilbert Gaul.

Battles and Leaders of the Civil War

near Richmond), but was not feasible when the battles occurred in distant rural areas.

The Union armies had the services of Thaddeus Lowe, who had invented a portable field generator to make hydrogen by which his balloons could be inflated. He provided valuable service to the Federal forces on more than one occasion. During George McClellan's Peninsula Campaign of 1862, Lowe often sent back word of Confederate troop positions by means of a telegraph wire extended from his balloon to the ground. At least one Union officer credited Lowe's observation with saving the entire army from destruction at Seven Pines.[3]

The use of balloons had drawbacks, particularly the vulnerability of the craft to high winds and bad weather. Political friction between the military organization and Lowe's civilian balloon corps led to the disuse of Union balloons by mid-1863.

In summary, then, a Civil War commander looked mainly to couriers on horseback to deliver orders and to send back information. As mentioned previously, the time delay associated with this method when used on a large battlefield could be a significant problem. How were two subordinate commanders to be able to attack the enemy simultaneously when they were out of sight of one another? How could the overall commander know exactly when and where to send in reinforcements without a time delay of such length that the moment was lost?

The answer was sound. Though not nearly as fast as light, sound could travel through one mile of air in about five seconds. This was not instantaneous, but certainly much faster than any horse.

An experienced officer could follow the course of a battle to some extent merely by listening to the sounds. Personal recollections of those who lived through the battles rarely fail to mention the sounds associated with the different phases of the fighting. As an example, here are some excerpts from E. P. Alexander's memoirs of the fighting at First Manassas:

- "Meanwhile, quite a fire of both musketry and artillery was beginning to develop on the left, where McDowell's advance had now come in collision with Evans's little force."[4]
- "The roar of the young battle now swelled in volume. There came crashes of musketry which told that whole brigades were coming in, and the fire of the guns increased."[5]

✗ "I was able to follow the progress of the battle by the rising clouds of smoke and the gradual approach of the musketry for an hour or two…"[6]

✗ "About 11.30 A.M., Stevens having gone less than a half-hour, there came a further access of fire both of musketry and artillery. It was doubtless due to the attack of Sherman and Keyes upon the flank of Bee and Bartow. No one who heard it could doubt its import. No messages from the left were needed now. All paused for a moment and listened. Then Johnston said, "The battle is there! I am going." Walking rapidly to his horse, he mounted and set off at a gallop, followed by his own staff, as fast as they could get their horses. "Beauregard only paused long enough to give a few brief orders. Holmes's and Early's brigades, and two regiments of Bonham's with Walker's and Kemper's batteries, were to march to the firing. Jones's brigade was to be recalled to our side of Bull Run."[7]

Even a cursory reading of the vast Civil War literature provides many examples of commanders interpreting the course of a battle from its sounds. The last excerpt above also shows another way in which acoustic signals were used: to send reinforcements to the point where the sounds of battle were the "hottest." A quick decision based in this way could save crucial minutes otherwise lost to couriers.

Here's another example, this from Gaines's Mill. These are Thomas J. "Stonewall" Jackson's instructions to a staff officer, also recorded by Alexander:

> The troops are standing at ease along our line of march. Ride back rapidly along the line, and tell the commanders to advance instantly in echelon from the left. Each brigade is to follow as a guide, the right regiment of the brigade on the left, and to keep within supporting distance. Tell the commanders if this formation fails at any point, to form line of battle and move to the front, pressing to the sound of the heaviest firing, and attack the enemy vigorously wherever found…[8]

Another way in which sound was used during the war was as a signal for action. To synchronize forces so that they might act simultaneously, a commander's strategy would sometimes call for one subordinate to begin a troop movement when the sounds of action by another unit was heard. We will see examples of such strategy failing at both Iuka and Seven Pines. Another example from the Seven Days' battles:

> Huger's four brigades, about 9000 men, were advancing down the Charles City road, and were expected to open the action on this part of the field at an early hour. Either his guns or Jackson's would be the signal for Longstreet and A. P. Hill to take up the battle.[9]

These orders by Robert E. Lee also failed, for the simple reason that the two subordinate commanders (Benjamin Huger and Stonewall Jackson) failed to begin the battle. At Iuka and Seven Pines, however, the "sound as a signal" strategy should have worked. In both cases, the battles began somewhat as planned, but the commander waiting for the acoustic signal didn't hear it. These failures were the work of acoustic shadows.

Civil War commanders relied heavily on their sense of hearing in their planning and conduct of battle. We know from chapter 2 that sound can do strange things outdoors; a person can be fairly close to a loud sound source and not hear it. What happened if a commander was depending on the sounds of battle and unknowingly placed himself in an acoustic shadow? The remainder of this book looks at that question in some detail.

Chapter 4

Fort Donelson, Tennessee

Ulysses S. Grant's triumph at Fort Donelson brought him national attention and respect. Unusual acoustics, however, almost kept him from achieving his first great victory.

Background

In the fall of 1861, President Abraham Lincoln drew up a "Memorandum for a Plan of Campaign" in which he specified his grand vision for the conduct of the war in the short term.[1] Lincoln's plan consisted of a three-pronged attack centered on Virginia. Forces under Major General George B. McClellan would attack towards Richmond from the north (or, as it turned out, from the east, up the James River Peninsula), while other Union troops advanced from Kentucky and Ohio into eastern Tennessee, and an amphibious force landed in eastern North Carolina.

The attack on eastern Tennessee was to be carried out by about 45,000 troops under Brigadier General Don Carlos Buell, in command of the Union's Department of the Ohio. McClellan advised Buell in January of 1862 that "my own advance cannot, according to my present views, be made until your troops are soundly established to the eastern portion of Tennessee."[2] By occupying eastern Tennessee, and particularly Cumberland Gap at the Tennessee-Virginia border, Union forces would control the railroad connecting Virginia to the West. This would help to prevent the Confederates from making use of their interior lines in reinforcing against McClellan's drive towards Richmond.

At least as important, in Lincoln's mind, was that occupation of eastern Tennessee would provide relief for the largely pro-Union population there. Securing the area would provide a wedge between the eastern and western parts of the Confederacy.

For a number of reasons, including inexperience in the ranks and rugged terrain, Buell was slow to start his advance. This delay provided an opportunity for Major General Henry Halleck to make his mark. The ambitious and politically minded Halleck had no desire to spend the war as commander of an unimportant backwater army. He had a plan that would give his Department of the Mississippi more significance than McClellan, now in charge of all Union forces, and the War Department officials attributed to it.

Why not, he suggested to McClellan, strike into the Confederate heartland by the most direct route possible? The Confederate advance line in the West ran through southern Kentucky from Bowling Green over to Columbus on the Mississippi River. Halleck's proposed movement would sever the Confederate defenses. An attacking force moving down the easily navigable Tennessee and Cumberland Rivers could quickly get as far south as Mississippi and Alabama on the former and straight into Nashville on the latter. The attack would have the added benefit of cutting an important Confederate railroad, the Memphis and Ohio, which crossed the Cumberland River at Clarksville.

Foreseeing such an attack, the Confederates had constructed two forts just below the Kentucky-Tennessee border: Fort Henry on the Tennessee River and Fort Donelson on the Cumberland. Fort Henry, although placed on low ground, commanded a long straight stretch of the Tennessee River. The winter rains of 1861–1862 had put the fort under a couple of feet of high water. The fort was an earthen work, with 12 guns facing the river and five more guarding the land approaches. Fort Donelson, 12 miles to the east of Fort Henry, was much stronger. Also constructed of earth, it was more than one hundred feet above the Cumberland River. Situated near a bend in the river, any approaching gunboats would be easy prey for the fort's batteries.

While Lincoln and McClellan still ascribed more importance to eastern Tennessee than to Halleck's theatre of operations, the news in January of the impending transfer of Confederate General P.G.T.

Fig. 4.1. Henry Halleck

Library of Congress

Beauregard to the West helped sway them in deciding to let Halleck carry out his plan. Officials in Washington mistakenly thought that Beauregard was bringing 15 regiments with him, and if Halleck was going to move it might be best to do so before the new Confederates arrived.[3] The fact that any sort of success on his part would give him a chance to ascend over the dawdling Buell to overall command in the West could not have escaped Halleck. On January 30, 1862, Halleck gave orders for an attack on Fort Henry. At the time, Halleck believed Fort Donelson to be a weak outpost of Fort Henry.

Halleck was not a well-liked general, perceived as a man who would not take responsibility for his failures and would claim responsibility for the successes of others. This aspect of his character would become more obvious later in the war in his position of Union general in chief. He was an intellectual general who had been given the somewhat derisive nickname "Old Brains." To lead the attack on the two river forts, Halleck chose a man different from him in many ways.

Ulysses S. Grant's record in the war to this point had not been stellar, with a costly draw at Belmont on the Mississippi River being his only command experience. He also had a reputation as a heavy drinker. But he was a tough and quiet man, and his straightforward demeanor was a stark contrast to Halleck's calculating nature. The attack on the two river forts would bring Grant to the attention of the nation and would be the beginning of a career that would far eclipse Halleck's.

Working in concert with Grant would be Commodore Andrew H. Foote, flag officer of a flotilla of gunboats. The flotilla consisted of three conventional wooden ships and four brand new ironclad gunboats, the *Cincinnati*, the *Carondelet*, the *St. Louis,* and the *Essex*. They were slow and ugly, but well armed. The first three ironclads each had 13 guns: three on the bow, two on the stern, and four on each broadside. The boats would soon prove their worth.

Grant's troops were at Cairo, Illinois, where the Ohio River joins the Mississippi. By February 3, his men had been loaded onto transports and had worked their way up the Ohio and onto the Tennessee River. By the night of February 4, most of Grant's men (under the immediate command of Brigadier General John A. McClernand) had disembarked on the eastern bank of the Tennessee, about four miles above Fort Henry. The force consisted of nine infantry regiments, two cavalry regiments, and four batteries of artillery. The transports headed back to the Ohio to pick up more troops while Grant went up the river with Foote to probe the fort with fire from the gunboats (in the theatre of Grant's operations, both the Cumberland and Tennessee run to the north).

The Confederates had planted torpedoes in the river, but the high water had washed most of them away. Though the exchange of fire was inconclusive, it gave Grant a chance to scrutinize the lay of the land and formulate a plan.

He ordered McClernand to move out at 11 A.M. on February 6, seize the road leading from Fort Henry to Fort Donelson, and prepare to assault Fort Henry. Transports brought more troops up the Tennessee, these under Brigadier General Charles F. Smith, and Grant had them land on the western bank of the river. He ordered Smith to seize the high ground across the river from Fort Henry.

Fort Henry was under the command of Brigadier General Lloyd Tilghman. After observing the buildup of opposing forces, Tilghman correctly decided that it

Fig. 4.2. Ulysses S. Grant

National Archives

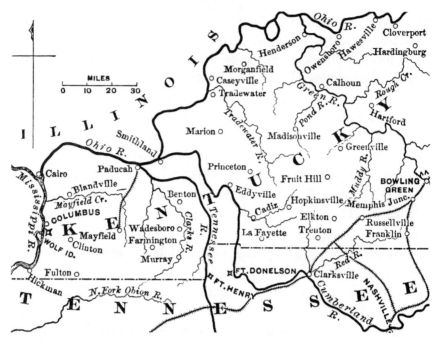

Fig. 4.3. The Bowling Green-Columbus Line

Force, *From Fort Henry to Corinth*

would be folly to risk the loss of his entire force by defending the fort. Upon assuming command of the place, he had disgustedly remarked on the poor choice of site for it. "The history of military engineering records no parallel to this case," he said and added that the fort was "without one redeeming feature."[4] On the night of February 5, he decided to keep only enough men in the fort to man the guns and to send the rest to Fort Donelson, where they might stand a chance. Most of the men made good their escape before McClernand's men could intercept them.

At 11:45 A.M. on February 6, Foote's gunboats had closed to within about a mile of the fort and the battle began. At first, the Confederate artillerists (with Tilghman himself eventually working a gun) held their own. Most of their shots bounced off the ironclads, but one managed to get through the plating to blow up the boiler of the *Essex*, scalding 28 men and killing the pilot at the wheel. But Foote cut the range in half, and the accurate fire of his boats soon took its toll within the fort. Four guns and their crews were put out of action, and at 1:55 P.M. Tilghman lowered the fort's flag.

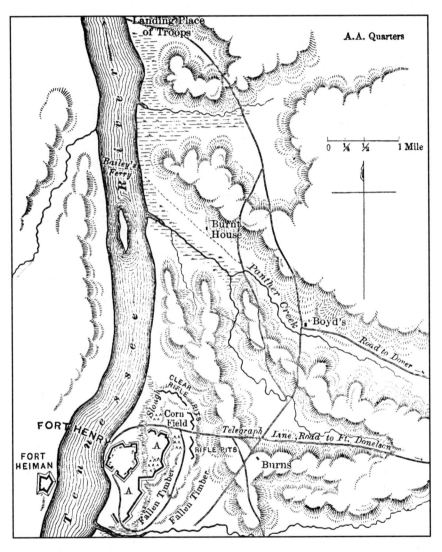

Fig. 4.4. Fort Henry, Tennessee

Force, *From Fort Henry to Corinth*

Grant wired Halleck, giving him news of the victory. He also informed him that he would continue on and "take and destroy Fort Donelson on the 8th."[5] Again, at this point, both Grant and Halleck assumed that Fort Henry had been the stronger of the two forts.

Grant's initial estimate of February 8 proved to be optimistic, as there was work to be done before proceeding to Fort Donelson. The three wooden gunships continued up the Tennessee to wreak havoc on the railroad bridges crossing the river while Foote returned to Cairo to repair the fleet. On the night of February 11, Grant finally began to move his army towards Fort Donelson. Also on the eleventh, Foote left Cairo with a new group of armored ships, the *Cincinnati* and the *Essex* not being repaired in time. Reinforcements arrived at Fort Henry on February 12, but Grant ordered them to stay on their troop transports and travel back down the Tennessee, up the Ohio, and then up the Cumberland to Fort Donelson.

As the men made their way across the muddy roads between the two rivers, the weather turned unseasonably warm. Many of the inexperienced troops acted as if the march had become a spring stroll, discarding their blankets, overcoats, and even their knapsacks by the side of the road. Within 36 hours, they would regret their actions.

Over at Fort Donelson, there was confusion. On the night of February 6, the garrison (under Brigadier General Bushrod R. Johnson) numbered about six thousand men, including the refugees from Fort Henry.[6] The Confederate high command in Bowling Green was faced with a difficult decision. Generals Albert Sidney Johnston and P.G.T. Beauregard (who had arrived there on the fourth) and Brigadier General William J. Hardee all agreed that Fort Donelson could not be held by its current force. It also seemed wise to give up Kentucky, at least temporarily, and withdraw to a more compact line around Nashville now that the Bowling Green-Columbus line of defense had been penetrated. But should Fort Donelson be strengthened to protect Nashville or should it be left alone while most of the troops retreated?

Johnston, in overall command, made a decision that still confuses historians. By reinforcing Fort Donelson with most of his troops, he might have taken care of Grant and then turned on the slow-moving Buell. But his men were spread far apart along the line of defense.

Approximately 14,000 were at Bowling Green and 17,000 at Columbus, with smaller forces spread in between. In addition to the force at Fort Donelson, there were about eight thousand men under Brigadier Generals John B. Floyd and Simon Bolivar Buckner at Russellville, two thousand under Brigadier General Charles Clark at Hopkinsville, and two thousand with Brigadier General Gideon J. Pillow at Clarksville.[7]

Instead of gathering his forces at Fort Donelson, Johnston sent the smaller forces there and ordered the two larger forces to retreat towards Nashville. He sent Beauregard to supervise the retreat from Columbus. Though soldiers on both sides of the war had high regard for Johnston, Grant was not impressed. As he wrote later: "After studying the orders and dispatches of Johnston, I am compelled to materially modify my views of that officer's qualifications as a soldier."[8]

By February 12, the force at Fort Donelson consisted of about 18,000 troops, a cavalry regiment, and six light artillery batteries, in addition to the fixed water batteries on the riverside of the fort. Johnston gave the command to Floyd, with Pillow second in command. Events would show that neither was a competent military leader.

The van of Grant's army drove in the Confederate pickets and came in sight of Fort Donelson about noon on the twelfth.[9] By late on that day, Grant had placed his left wing under Smith opposite the Confederate right wing under Buckner and had his right wing under McClernand opposite the Confederate left wing under Pillow.

By morning of the thirteenth, Grant still did not know the whereabouts of the gunboat fleet (which was slowly fighting its way upstream against the current of the swollen Cumberland) and had 15,000 men, without supplies, facing a greater number of entrenched enemy soldiers. Though Grant gave orders to avoid battle that day, pending the arrival of reinforcements and the gunboats, several sporadic skirmishes broke out. Sharpshooters on both sides also began to ply their deadly trade.

It is hard now to understand why the Confederates did not attempt to break free from Grant's investment of their position on the thirteenth. The situation could only get worse with the arrival of more Federal soldiers or of the gunboats. But the Confederates did not attack.

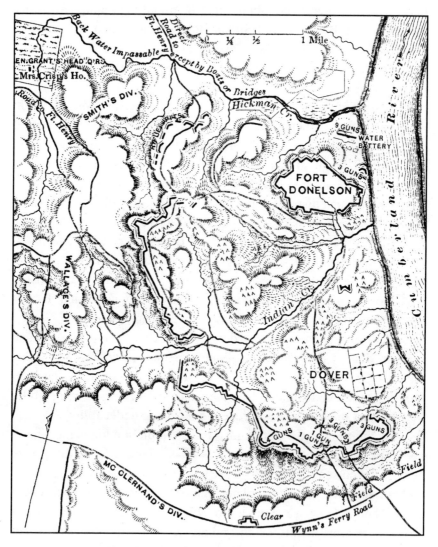

Fig. 4.5. Fort Donelson, Tennessee

Force, *From Fort Henry to Corinth*

By that night, soldiers on both sides probably wished they were somewhere else. The balmy weather suddenly turned chilly and the wind began to blow. By evening it began to rain and by 9:00 P.M. the rain had turned into a nasty mix of snow, sleet, and hail. The wind blew in furious gusts, and many a Union soldier must have longed for an overcoat discarded on the march over from Fort Henry. The temperature dropped to around 12 degrees Fahrenheit.

The gunboat *Carondelet* had arrived at Fort Donelson around noon on the twelfth, having not returned to Cairo with the other boats. Moored about four miles downstream from Fort Donelson, she was joined by the *St. Louis, Louisville,* and *Pittsburg* at about midnight on the thirteenth.[10] Grant rode to the landing on the morning of the fourteenth to confer with Foote and by early afternoon the gunboats were steaming up the Cumberland toward the fort. Grant had decided to see if the gunboats could overwhelm Fort Donelson the way that they had overwhelmed Fort Henry.

The first shots were fired between the gunboats and Fort Donelson's water batteries between 2:30 and 3:00 P.M. and soon solid shot and shell filled the air. By 3:30 P.M., the gunboats had worked their way to within four hundred yards of the batteries. At first it was not obvious who was doing more damage, but in the next half-hour it became clear that the

Fig. 4.6. Fort Donelson's Lower Water Battery

Lossing, *Pictorial Field Book of the Civil War*

Confederate gunners at Donelson were faring far better than had their counterparts at Fort Henry. The elevated position of the Confederate guns allowed their shots to strike the gunboat's sloping armor at almost a 90-degree angle instead of glancing off as at Fort Henry. Also, the Union gunners had trouble elevating their guns high enough to strike back at the Confederates.

Several Confederate shots disabled the *St. Louis*, one wounding Foote in the ankle, and the flagship drifted back downstream. The *Louisville* was also battered and lost her tiller. The *Pittsburg* had to retire when she began to take on water and accidentally slammed into the *Carondelet*.

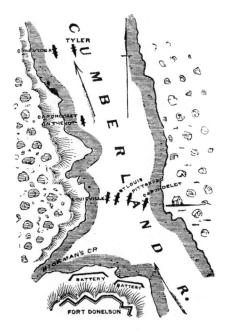

Fig. 4.7. Positions of the Gunboats in the Attack on Fort Donelson

Lossing, *Pictorial Field Book of the Civil War*

By 4:30 P.M. the fight was over and loud Confederate cheers rang through Fort Donelson. Grant must have felt frustrated. Despite having received substantial reinforcements from the troop transports that had accompanied the gunboats up the Cumberland, enough men to lock in the fort's defenders indefinitely, the prospect of a siege could not have been inviting. Luckily for Grant, the Confederate commanders would save him the trouble of planning a siege. Two days late, they decided to make their break.

Meeting late on the night of the fourteenth, Floyd, Pillow, and Buckner devised a plan that, if carried out to the letter, might have allowed them to extricate themselves from their predicament. Pillow was to assault the Union right just before daybreak and roll up McClernand's right flank. Buckner's men then would emerge from their trenches and attack the Union center. When the Union right and center had been pushed back far enough to clear the roads heading south,

Pillow's men would begin the retreat with Buckner holding the enemy back and then acting as rear guard on the march to join Johnston's men in Nashville.

Also on the night of the fourteenth, Grant received a note at 2:00 A.M. from Foote asking for a meeting. As Foote was still nursing his injury, he requested that Grant travel to meet him. Grant left on horseback, leaving instructions for his division commanders to hold their positions and not bring on an engagement unless ordered to do so. He left no one in overall command.

The Battle and the Acoustics

Sometime around dawn on February 15, the Confederates began their surprise attack on the Union right. The snow and thick brush made it tough going, but by 8:00 A.M. Pillow's men were firmly on McClernand's flank. McClernand sent two of his staff members racing to the Union left to plead for assistance. Brigadier General Lewis Wallace heard the somewhat muffled sounds of the battle but at first refused to send reinforcements until hearing from Grant.[11] Alerted that Grant was still away (with Foote) and sensing that disaster was imminent, Wallace took the responsibility and began to shift men towards the battered Union right.

At this point, Buckner brought his men out of their trenches and the fighting intensified. By late morning, the first part of the Confederate plan had been achieved. The Union right had been pushed back and the road south was clear for the retreat. Pillow sent a telegram to Johnston proclaiming that "On the honor of a soldier, the day is ours."[12]

As the battle raged, Grant was conferring with Foote aboard the *St. Louis*, about four miles north of the left flank of the Union position.[13] Foote informed Grant that he intended to take his fleet back to Illinois for repairs and advised Grant that he should plan on holding his position until the boats returned in about two weeks. This cannot have pleased the impatient Grant. Despite the success of the gunboats at Fort Henry, Grant still had faith in the army's ability to get the job done. But he wanted to avoid a siege if possible. In the end, Foote agreed to take only his two most damaged ships back down the river and leave the others to protect the transports and offer some supporting fire.

As Grant disembarked from the *St. Louis* around noon, the battle was six hours old. As he reached shore, one of his aides (Captain William S. Hillyer) galloped up with the news of the fight. This appeared to stun Grant somewhat, as he had not expected any serious fighting to occur unless he initiated it.[14] With Hillyer, he took off for the battlefield.

Why had Grant not returned earlier in the day to lead his men? The evidence points to an acoustic shadow. One would expect a battle of this magnitude to be audible at a distance of four miles, but such does not appear to have been the case. In the words of Lt. Colonel Manning F. Force of the 20th Ohio: "…there was nothing in the sound that came through several miles of intervening forest to indicate anything more serious than McClernand's previous assaults."[15] So whatever sounds made their way to Grant did not carry the full intensity of the fighting. In the words of Shelby Foote, "Baffled by the wintry trees and ridges, the three-hour uproar of Pillow's assault…reached him faintly, if at all."[16]

The many official reports of the battle indicate that the fighting on Saturday morning was of a much more intense character than the skirmishing of the previous two days. In the words of Lew Wallace, the night of February 14 was "quiet, broken at intervals by guns from the rebels."[17] He then describes the fighting of the next morning: "The firing was very heavy and continuous, being musketry and artillery mixed."[18] Other excerpts from official Union reports describing the battle on Saturday include: "terrific cannonade," "heavy fire of musketry," "an almost incessant discharge of musketry," "galling fire," and "the fire upon our lines continued with unabated fury."[19] If such sounds had reached Grant, the change from skirmish to battle would certainly have been obvious to him.

The conditions outdoors at the time were ripe for poor acoustics. The storm that began on the night of February 13 must have been awful, as almost every personal recollection of the battle describes it and the subsequent suffering of the men on both sides. The storm brought both snow and wind, both potential killers of sound. Descriptions include "a driving north wind bringing a storm of snow and sleet"; "a storm of rain, soon turning to snow and accompanied by severe blasts"; and "one of the most persecuting snow-storms ever known in this country."[20]

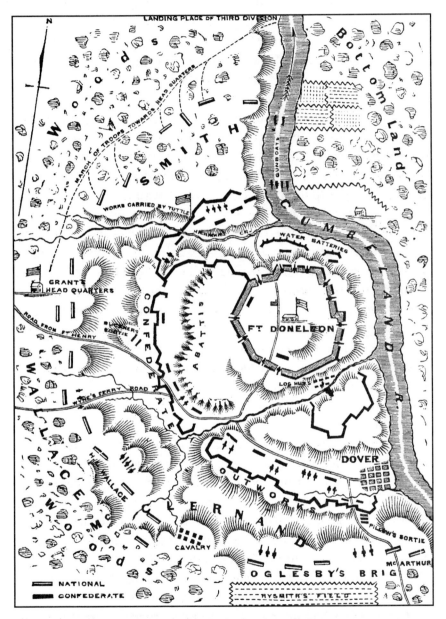

Fig. 4.8. Plan of the Siege of Fort Donelson

Lossing, *Pictorial Field Book of the Civil War*

Though the precipitation ended by Saturday morning, the winds appear to have persisted through Saturday night.[21] It is important to note that the wind was out of the north, the direction in which Grant had moved from the battlefield. In such an upwind position, it would be difficult to hear sounds four miles distant if the winds were as strong as described.

The ground and the foliage were covered with a three-inch blanket of fresh snow, offering the potential for sound absorption.[22] Even without the high winds and the snow cover, the terrain was not very conducive to the propagation of sound. Some descriptions of the land include: "very rolling and thickly covered with timber," "very hilly and thickly wooded," and "the bushes were very thick."[23]

Given the type of terrain, the snow cover, and the wind, Grant could hardly have chosen a worse spot to be for hearing the battle. Sounds did not seem to be carrying well in any direction on the morning of the fifteenth, however. The sounds of the Confederate mobilization for the assault appear not to have reached the Union lines, adding to the surprise of the attack. In the words of a Union officer: "It seems incomprehensible that columns mixed of all arms, infantry, cavalry, and artillery, could have engaged in simultaneous movement and not have been heard by some listener outside. But the character of the night must be remembered. The pickets of the Federals were struggling for life against the blast..."[24]

Grant arrived back at the battlefield at about 1:00 P.M. He quickly analyzed the deteriorating situation. If the Confederates were mounting such a strong attack from their left, they must have weakened their right. A counterattack there might turn the battle around. Accordingly, he ordered Brigadier General Smith to attack the Confederate right. Smith's men at first encountered little opposition and quickly gained the outer breastworks of the Confederate position.

Grant was now aided by confusion among the Confederate command. While the Union troops had spent the morning without a leader, the Confederates had more leaders than they needed. Just at the point when escape might have been made, Pillow decided that retreat was in order. He thus ordered the furious Buckner back into the trenches. Many of Buckner's men returned to their original positions and stemmed the tide of Smith's attack, but the Confederate moment had passed. Bloody fighting continued on this side of the field for the remainder of the afternoon. Floyd, ostensibly in charge of the Confederates, appears to have had no control over the action.

Wallace and McClernand then, at Grant's urging, fought back and regained the ground lost to Pillow during the morning. The exhausted Confederates retired back into their fortifications.

The Aftermath

Grant had certainly arrived back to the field in the nick of time. Acoustic shadows had almost caused him to miss out on his first great victory. It would certainly have been an embarrassing defeat.

On the night of the fifteenth, the Confederate commanders held what must have been an extraordinary meeting. At first, Pillow was all for making another attempt at cutting their way out, and was firmly seconded by cavalry Colonel Nathan Bedford Forrest. But Buckner had turned defeatist and eventually convinced the others (except Forrest) that escape was impossible. Floyd and Pillow then decided that, though they would surrender their men, they had no intention of sharing their fate. Floyd looked at Pillow and said, "I turn the command over, sir," and Pillow then turned to Buckner and said, "I pass it." Buckner, apparently willing to play the martyr, replied, "I assume it." On a day of indecision in the Confederate high ranks, someone was finally willing to take responsibility.

During the night, Pillow escaped across the river while Floyd commandeered a steamer just arriving with four hundred unlucky recruits from Mississippi. He left the new men on shore while ferrying himself across, along with much of his brigade. Forrest led about five hundred cavalrymen out by fording a creek between the Union right flank and the river. Shortly before daybreak, Buckner sent a contingent across to the Union lines asking for terms of surrender.

Grant replied: "No terms except unconditional and immediate surrender can be accepted. I propose to move immediately upon your works."[25] Buckner had no choice but to accept. Grant fired off a telegram to Halleck, announcing the victory. The news brought jubilation to the north and Grant's initials quickly came to stand for "Unconditional Surrender." Fort Donelson, the battle he almost lost due to acoustics, was the first step in Grant's road to fame.

The captured Confederates were shipped to Northern prison camps, and Grant and Halleck turned their thoughts southward. The opening of the Tennessee and Cumberland Rivers did indeed open up the middle of the Confederacy. Grant would win another hard victory in April 1862 at Shiloh, and the Confederate line, once stretched across Kentucky, would continue to bend backwards. In the fall of 1862 the action would reach Mississippi, where Grant would experience another acoustic shadow, one that would rob him of a victory.

Chapter 5

Seven Pines, Virginia

The drawn battle at Seven Pines would almost certainly have been a Confederate victory if not for mismanagement among the generals in gray. An acoustic shadow appears to have added to the confusion and caused a sequence of events that brought Robert E. Lee into command.

Background

While Ulysses Grant showed early signs of his blunt and direct approach to fighting at Forts Henry and Donelson, events in the east proved to be less straightforward. Major General George McClellan had taken over command of all Union forces in the fall of 1861, a few months after the debacle at Bull Run. During the last months of 1861 and the beginning of 1862, McClellan breathed new life into the forces in blue, instilling discipline and spirit where defeatism had prevailed.

By the time Grant had succeeded at Fort Donelson, President Abraham Lincoln was pleased with McClellan's work but also anxious that he turn from training to fighting. Public opinion in the North demanded retribution for Bull Run and for the disaster at Ball's Bluff in October 1861. According to Lincoln, "…if General McClellan did not want to use the army, he would like to borrow it, provided he could see how it could be made to do something."[1]

Lincoln favored a direct attack on the Confederates still encamped at Manassas. The Union forces numbered now close to two hundred thousand while the Confederates had barely more than 50,000. McClellan favored turning the Confederate position by moving his forces by boat down to the Rappahannock River at Urbana, 40 miles east of

Richmond and 90 miles southeast of Johnston's line at Manassas. With the support of his generals, McClellan was able to gain permission from Lincoln (provided that the safety of Washington was assured) for his plan, though Lincoln never believed it to be superior to his own.

The cautious Johnston, sensing danger, began to withdraw southward from Manassas in early March to a point just south of the Rappahannock. McClellan adjusted his plan accordingly, and on March 17 an enormous flotilla left the Potomac. The boats were headed now for Fort Monroe, on the James River Peninsula.

The last week of March was spent organizing men and equipment, and on April 4 the Union forces started up the peninsula. The only opposition to McClellan's enormous army was a force of about 11,000 Confederates at Yorktown under Brigadier General John B. Magruder. During the next week, Johnston hurried men down the Peninsula until the number at Yorktown had risen to about 30,000 men. With the help of slaves and civilians, the Confederates threw up breastworks in McClellan's path.

The cautious McClellan moved slowly and decided to subject Yorktown to a siege. For several weeks, Union heavy guns bombarded the Confederates, but without much effect. Johnston, however, had decided that the Yorktown position was ultimately untenable and vulnerable to being flanked by forces moving up the York or James Rivers. He convinced the unhappy Jefferson Davis that retreat was in order, though this would mean losing the Norfolk Shipyard as well as Yorktown. On May 4, Union pickets found the Confederate lines at Yorktown to be empty.

McClellan began an immediate pursuit, and later that day his advance caught up with the Confederate rear guard at Williamsburg. Early the next morning a sharp little battle began and lasted until evening on April 5. When McClellan and his men looked to the Confederate lines at daybreak on the sixth, they were empty again. This time McClellan, waiting for his supply trains to catch up, slowed the pursuit.

Johnston continued his retreat and ended up much too close to Richmond for Davis's liking. By mid-May, Johnston was setting up his men in a defensive arc around Richmond, about 15 miles long and only about five miles from the outskirts of the city. McClellan followed, and ended up facing Johnston, but with part of his army north of the Chickahominy River and part of it on the south side. This precarious arrangement was made partially because McClellan expected even more men to be coming to his assistance. Almost 40,000 men under Brigadier General Irvin McDowell had been ordered southward from Manassas. They were to keep themselves between any Confederates and the nation's capital, but link their left wing with McClellan's right wing north of the Chickahominy.

On May 24, Johnston heard of McDowell's movement, and he knew that his army had to go on the offensive.[2] This was an anathema to the cautious Johnston, but if McDowell was able to join McClellan it would be disaster. He decided to attack the Union right wing before McDowell could arrive. Here McClellan had placed his best troops, the V Corps under Brigadier General Fitz John Porter and the VI Corps under Brigadier General William B. Franklin. South of the river, where he expected little likelihood of action, McClellan had placed troops (and commanders) in which he had less confidence: the IV Corps under Major General Erasmus D. Keyes and the III Corps under Major General Samuel P. Heintzelman. Just north of the river and serving to connect the III and IV Corps with the V and VI Corps was the II Corps under Major General Edwin V. Sumner.

Johnston had informed Davis of his plans to attack. When word reached Johnston that Stonewall Jackson's successes in the Shenandoah Valley had prompted McDowell to turn back northward, he still felt pressure from Davis to attack McClellan. He now decided to go after what he felt was McClellan's weakest point, the IV Corps, which had advanced to a country intersection known as Seven Pines. He devised a plan in which most of his men would attack McClellan's left wing, while the others stood guard to prevent reinforcements from moving across the Chickahominy.

Johnston's original plan, a good one, was aided by a tremendous thunderstorm on May 30, the day before the scheduled attack. This caused the Chickahominy to become severely flooded and isolated the two Union corps on the south side of the river from the rest of the army. Johnston's strategy would make good use of the location of Seven Pines. The Williamsburg Road headed directly through Seven Pines from Richmond, while the Nine Mile Road moved in an arc to the north before dipping southeast and intersecting the Williamsburg Road at Seven Pines. The Nine Mile Road continued southward until it terminated at the Charles City Road, which ran in an east-west direction a few miles south of the Williamsburg Road.

The first Union line of defense was located about a half mile to the west of Seven Pines along the Williamsburg Road. Here McClellan had inexplicably located some of the greenest troops in the army, under Brigadier General Silas Casey. Behind this was another line at Seven Pines.[3] The defensive fortifications that had been constructed there were not particularly strong.

Johnston's army was divided into three wings. The right wing was commanded by Major General James Longstreet and consisted of his own division of six brigades and four additional brigades under Major General Daniel Harvey Hill. The center wing was commanded by Major General Gustavus W. Smith and consisted of four brigades under Major General Ambrose Powell Hill and Smith's own division of five brigades (temporarily under Brigadier General William Henry Chase Whiting). The left wing consisted of two brigades under Major General David R. Jones and four brigades under Major General Lafayette McLaws. Johnston also had at his disposal a cavalry brigade under Brigadier General James Ewell Brown (J.E.B.) Stuart and three brigades of infantry under Major General Benjamin Huger. Huger's men had retreated from Norfolk after the fall of that city and had been most recently at Drewry's Bluff on the south side of the James River.

While the left wing and part of the center (the brigades under A. P. Hill) kept an eye on the Union troops north of the Chickahominy, the rest of the Confederates would converge on Seven Pines along the Williamsburg and Nine Mile Roads. One problem facing Johnston was that one of D. H. Hill's brigades (under Brigadier General Robert E. Rodes) was presently on the Charles City Road. To get Hill's men back together, Johnston decided to replace Rodes's troops with Huger's.

So, the original plan of attack was as follows. Huger's men were to march down the Charles City Road and relieve Rodes's troops. Rodes would then march across the wooded countryside to join Hill on the Williamsburg Road. Rodes's arrival would let Hill know that his right

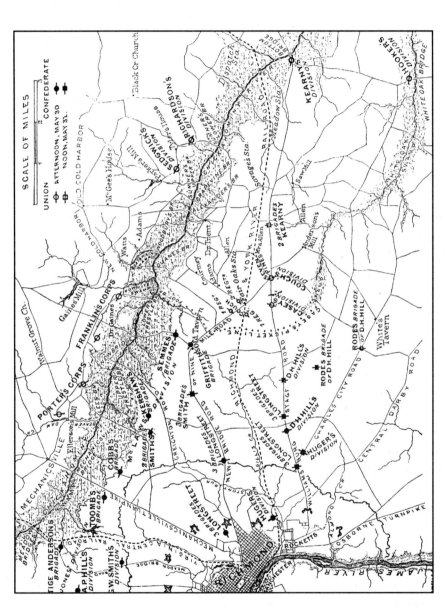

Fig. 5.1. Positions before the Battle of Seven Pines

flank was secure and Hill would begin the attack. The sound of his guns would alert Longstreet to begin attacking down the Nine Mile Road. The attack was to begin shortly after daybreak (about 4:00 A.M.) and Johnston expected that the battle would be in full swing before 8:00 A.M.[4] Johnston made his headquarters a short way out on the Nine Mile Road from Richmond.

At about 6:00 A.M., Whiting's men (who were to act as reserve for Longstreet) found their movement eastward on the Nine Mile Road blocked not far out of the Richmond suburbs by Longstreet's troops. When told of this, Johnston would not believe it as he thought Longstreet's men would be far down the road towards Seven Pines by this time. What he didn't know was that, due to a misunderstanding (Johnston apparently gave Longstreet no written orders) or to insubordination, Longstreet had decided to move his men westward on the Nine Mile Road and follow Hill's troops up the Williamsburg Road. In doing so he caused massive confusion, because his troops not only held up Whiting, but also blocked Huger from getting to the Charles City Road. With Huger held up, D. H. Hill continued to wait for Rodes (who was waiting for Huger) so that he could begin the battle.

As the morning wore on, Hill became more and more agitated. He finally sent orders to Rodes to move up to join him even though Huger was not yet in place. At about 1:00 P.M., the first men in Rodes's brigade emerged from the woods. Hill ordered Rodes to get them into line of battle facing eastward and march toward the Union line. He told Rodes to line up each regiment behind the other as they popped out of the woods. Rodes's men would be followed by troops under Brigadier General Gabriel J. Rains. On the north side of the road, a brigade under Brigadier General Samuel Garland, Jr., led the attack, backed by George Anderson's brigade. Hill fired his signal cannon and the attack began.

During the morning, the confused Johnston had moved his headquarters farther out the Nine Mile Road to Old Tavern, where the road dipped to the southeast and another road led northward to the Chickahominy. When it became obvious around 11:00 A.M. that things had gone seriously awry, Johnston said that "He wished the troops were all back in their camps."[5] Except for Whiting's troops, who had moved out to Old Tavern also, Johnston had little information as to the whereabouts of any of his men, and it appeared that a battle would not be fought that day after all. As the morning turned into afternoon, Johnston continued to believe that miscommunication had prevented his planned attack from occurring. Even by 4:00 P.M., Johnston still did not believe that a battle was being fought close by.

The Battle and the Acoustics

There is no doubt, however, that by 1:30 P.M. a battle was raging just to the west of Seven Pines and not far from Johnston's headquarters. There is also no doubt that many observers heard the battle at a variety of locations, as will be shown shortly. What is in question is what did Joseph Johnston hear and when did he hear it? If we can believe Johnston's account, the sounds of a furious battle did not reach him clearly though he was only about three miles from the heart of the fighting. This acoustic shadow, if real, had a major impact on the outcome at Seven Pines.

After the firing of the signal guns, the troops in Garland's brigade began to work their way through and out of the dense woods, with much difficulty. The Federal skirmishers of the 85th Pennsylvania fell back into the men of the 103rd Pennsylvania and a chaotic moving fight began. As the Union soldiers began to retreat in the face of Hill's overwhelming numbers, men on both sides became entangled in vines and thick brush or sank down to their hips into the marshy, flooded ground. Men suffering minor wounds drowned before they could be helped.

As they cleared the woods, the Pennsylvanians struggled back through their own abatis, 40 feet thick and constructed of felled trees. About two hundred yards behind the abatis, Casey deployed infantry and Battery H of the 1st New York Artillery with four three-inch rifled guns. The thick woods had thrown the Confederates into disorder also, and they approached the abatis with their lines in a mess. As Anderson's men came through the woods behind Garland's, they added to the confusion. It took until about 1:30 P.M. to recover some semblance of order in the lines.

South of the Williamsburg Road, Rodes was somewhat behind Garland and Anderson due to the piecemeal nature of his attack. As his men popped out of the White Oak Swamp, he hurried them to the

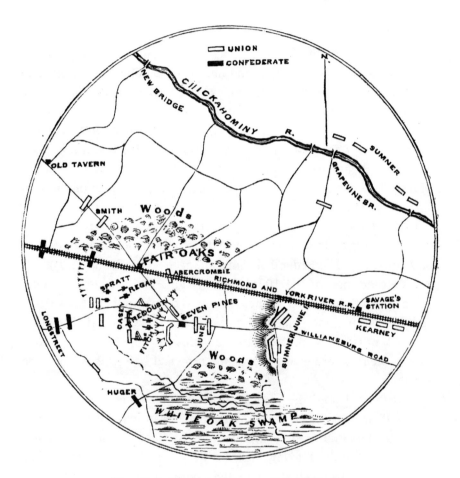

Fig. 5.2. Seven Pines and Fair Oaks

Lossing, *Pictorial Field Book of the Civil War*

front. By 2:00 P.M., Rodes's men had fought their way even with their comrades north of the road and the attack resumed in unison. As the Confederates swarmed through the abatis, Casey dropped his men several hundred yards farther back to the next line of defense.

Here were rifle pits and a pentagonal redoubt. In the redoubt, Casey had placed the guns of another battery, with a second battery to the far right of the rifle pits and a third behind the redoubt in reserve. Keyes had pushed up two additional regiments to reinforce Casey. Still, it was not enough. After bitter fighting, Hill's men began to push through the rifle pits on both sides of the road and the Union men fell back again, this time to a second line of defense at Seven Pines.

But the steamroller could not continue. The constant progress had come at heavy cost for Hill's men, with both Anderson's and Garland's brigades suffering heavy casualty rates.[6] Hill was reduced to using the brigades of Rodes and now Rains, who had joined Rodes from behind, to try and carry the next Union line. Less than half of the men with which Hill started his attack (and all of these south of the Williamsburg Road) would try to finish it.[7]

Heintzelman and Keyes rushed to plug gaps and strengthen their lines with reinforcements. When the fighting resumed at the Union second line, it was brutal and lasted throughout the late afternoon. The diminished Confederate force was not strong enough to complete the final push, and when darkness ended the fighting at Seven Pines the Union men could be pushed back no farther. Both the Union III and IV Corps had been decimated and the survival of the Union position had been in doubt until the end of the day.

In retrospect, one must wonder what would have been the effect of Confederate forces sweeping

Fig. 5.3. Joseph Johnston

Miller, *The Photographic History of the Civil War*

Fig. 5.4.
James Longstreet

Library of Congress

Fig. 5.5.
George McClellan

National Archives

down the Nine Mile Road from the north? Johnston's original plan would almost certainly have swept the Union IV Corps away easily and would probably have ended in a resounding victory south of the river. Still, even in light of Longstreet's insubordination, Johnston retained the chance for a clear-cut win at Seven Pines. Even after posting two of Smith's (Whiting's) brigades to watch the river crossings, he had three fresh brigades at Old Tavern. Sending these men down the Nine Mile Road at any point in the early afternoon would have meant a dramatic change in the course of the battle. Why did Johnston not send them in?

To answer the question, we can turn to Johnston's own writings:

> Owing to some peculiar condition of the atmosphere the sound of the musketry did not reach us. I consequently deferred the signal for General Smith's advance until about 4 o'clock.[8]

Also:

> When the action just described began, the musketry was not heard at my position on the Nine-mile road, from the unfavorable condition of the air; and I supposed for some time that we were hearing only an artillery duel. But a staff-officer was sent to ascertain the facts. He returned at 4 o'clock with intelligence that our infantry as well as artillery had been engaged an hour, and all were pressing on vigorously.[9]

Johnston's observations seem to be corroborated by Major General Smith, who was with Johnston at Old Tavern:

> The anxiety felt by those near Old Tavern was extreme in the hours of suspense previous to 4 P.M., during which all were expecting to hear that the fighting on the Williamsburg road had commenced. In my official report it is stated that 'as the day wore on and nothing decisive was heard from General Longstreet's attack, except occasional firing of cannon, and, for some two or three hours, but little musketry, it seemed that no real attack was likely to be made that day.' Previous to 4 P.M. it was believed by all on the Nine-mile road that no attack had yet been made; the division on that road could not be advanced beyond McLaw's picket-line without bringing on the battle which General Johnston intended should be initiated by the divisions of Hill and Longstreet.[10]

Douglas Southall Freeman describes the sounds heard at Old Tavern as a "vague undertone" of distant muskets that Johnston would refuse to attribute to a battle. The sounds were "now caught by keen ears, now dismissed as imaginary."[11] It appears that Old Tavern was located in an acoustic shadow of the sounds from Hill's battle. Perhaps younger staff members were able to pick out the intermittent and higher pitched sounds of the musketry better than Johnston and Smith, but even to these young men the sounds must not have been conclusive. Other accounts state that Robert E. Lee, on his arrival at Old Tavern that afternoon, heard the musketry and tried to convince Johnston of its significance without success.[12] Jefferson Davis, who also rode out to Old Tavern that afternoon, stated that he heard firing while riding out the Nine Mile Road to Old Tavern.[13]

There is also no doubt that the sounds of the battle did carry in other directions. A number of officers in Sumner's Corps mentioned hearing the sounds of the battle in their official reports. Sumner's men were located near Tyler's farm on the north side of the Chickahominy. This camp, situated about the same distance (three miles) from the battle as Old Tavern, was located to the northeast of the fighting while Old Tavern was to the northwest. Some examples of observations by men on the other side of the Chickahominy:

Brigadier General Thomas Meagher: "On Saturday, May 31, early in the forenoon, we of the Second Brigade, Richardson's division, Sumner's corps *d'armee*, being encamped at Tyler's farm, heard considerable firing in front. This firing continuing to increase in rapidity and loudness during the day..."[14]

Brigadier General William French: "When the heavy firing at about 1 p.m. on the 31st of May was heard in out front, whilst in camp near Cold Harbor..."[15]

Lieutenant Colonel John Kimball, 15th Massachusetts Infantry: "At this time (3 p.m.) and for an hour previous very heavy firing was heard on the south side of the Chickahominy Creek."[16]

Brigadier General N.J.T. Dana: "About 1:30 o'clock p.m. of the first-mentioned date (May 31) heavy firing was heard at our camp at Dr. Tyler's, on the east side of the Chickahominy River."[17] Captain George W. Hazzard, Sumner's chief of artillery noted that "Firing at Casey's camp was heard." This was at 1:00 P.M.

Union cavalryman F. Colburn Adams: "At fifteen minutes to one o'clock our whole camp was startled by the sudden, crashing sound of infantry and the deep roar of cannon. It seemed as if twenty thousand infantry had discharged simultaneously and repeated in such rapid succession that it were impossible to count the volleys. And this rolling and crashing of the infantry and roar of artillery at once indicated the fierceness of the battle that had begun."[18]

McClellan, also north of the Chickahominy, apparently heard the sounds of the fighting and it was these sounds that prompted him to order Sumner's divisions into action.[19] Though the various Union accounts above differ slightly as to the time of the first reports, there is little doubt that the battle was heard loud and clear across the Chickahominy.

The battle was also heard to the east of the fighting. Heintzelman stated in his report: "About 1 p.m. I first heard firing, more than there had been for several days."[20] Union brigadier Darius Couch stated that he could hear general musketry at about 1:30 p.m.[21] Other remarks from officers in rear of Casey's division include: "...heard heavy firing in our front, where General Casey's division was encamped,"[22] and "seven companies...assembled...as soon as the firing in front was heard, at about 1:30 p.m."[23]

The sounds of battle were also heard to the southwest of the fighting, where Confederate Brigadier General Cadmus M. Wilcox had his men marching down the Charles City Road: "...firing then heard raging furiously off to our left front."[24] The audibility of the sounds at positions on the Charles City Road is corroborated by other accounts.[25] There are reports that many civilians in Richmond, about five miles to the west of the fighting, kept abreast of the afternoon's fighting by listening to the battle sounds.[26]

If one scans reports from the various compass directions surrounding Seven Pines, evidence points to the battle being audible in every direction except for the direction in which Johnston had placed himself. Edward Porter Alexander summarizes the situation in his classic book, *Military Memoirs of a Confederate*:

> Toward noon Johnston left his headquarters, which were on
> the Nine Mile road about three miles from Richmond, and took
> his position at a house near the fork of the Nine Mile and New

Bridge roads. His intention was to send Whiting's division down the Nine Mile road to cooperate with D. H. Hill's attack down the Williamsburg road.

By coincidence of bad luck, his right wing having lost several hours in the morning, his left wing lost about three hours in the afternoon. The signal for Whiting's advance was to be the sound of Hill's musketry on the Williamsburg road, two miles southeast, through a wooded country. This musketry began about one o'clock, and heard in the Federal lines, five miles northeast; also, near Richmond five miles west; but was not audible two miles to the northwest at the position occupied by Whiting's division and by Gen. Johnston.

Alexander adds a footnote: "Such phenomena, called acoustic shadows, are of common occurrence and are to be expected upon every battle-field, in *some* direction; especially in wooded localities. Here the intervening ground was moderately wooded. The artillery could be distinguished, but the amount of it was not great."[27]

So, if we accept that an acoustic shadow did occur, what was the cause? First, we must look to the terrain. The field around Seven Pines (except for the immediate vicinity of the fighting) was very heavily wooded. The foliage consisted of tall trees, interspersed with young oaks and heavy brush.[28] The entire area was marshy.[29] Colonel William Smith of the 49th Virginia said that he had to "make my way through a trackless forest, encountering almost every step brush, bramble and pond…"[30]

Major General Gustavus Smith described his men's charge late on the 31st as "under a deadly fire in a dense, entangled wood, struggling through the morass, covered with logs and thick bushes." He also states that his officers "were laboring under great disadvantages, the thickness of the woods and undergrowth and the smoke preventing them from seeing more than a very limited number of their men at any one time…"[31] Finally, he observes regarding the terrain that "…most of it, except the small open spaces at the earthworks, was densely wooded and swampy. The soil in all that region, when wet, is very spongy, making passage over it difficult even for infantry. In the dense woods the thick undergrowth is matted with tangled vines, and the luxuriant foliage, in the full bloom of spring, rendered it in many places impossible to distinguish objects ten paces distant."[32]

The woods were so thick that D. H. Hill ordered his men to tie white cloth around their hats before the battle in order to distinguish friend from foe.[33]

The ground in the area was level, and so the contours of the land were no hindrance to the propagation of sound.[34] The deluging rains of the previous day, however, had left the normally soft ground in terrible condition. Men found themselves in water up to their waists as they struggled through the woods, and the raging Chickahominy was 18 inches deep, two hundred yards inland from its normal banks.[35]

So, we have a good scenario for bad acoustics: thick foliage and soft, absorbent ground. The fact that artillery, but not musketry, was audible at Old Tavern is consistent with the interactions of the short wavelength, high-frequency musketry sounds with the foliage. Even enlisted men were aware of the possibility for unusual acoustics in this area. One Confederate soldier, recalling his experiences a month later during the Seven Days' battles not far from Seven Pines, wrote that "It often happened that in these dense woods and thickets of eastern Virginia the sound of battle was hardly, if at all, heard some miles distant, although often passing overhead and borne to regions far more remote."[36]

Still, the thick woods and flooded ground can't be the whole story, for these conditions extended in all directions from Seven Pines. And days before the battle, McClellan had written that he could hear the clocks striking in Richmond, so the acoustics in the area were not totally ruined by the land cover.[37]

While the terrain certainly contributed to Johnston's acoustic shadow, the main culprit may have been the weather. The conditions in the air must have been unusually turbulent. As with the thick woods, many soldiers remembered the violent thunderstorm of May 30 when telling their tale of Seven Pines.[38] Many called it the worst they had ever seen. This is significant when considering that many of the soldiers had a rural background and were especially in tune to the weather. The storm apparently dumped more than three inches of rain during its first two hours.[39]

In the words of Union cavalry officer F. Colburn Adams: "The morning of the 30th came in hot and sultry...and about noon heavy storm clouds rolled up in threatening masses and filled the heavens with darkness. Then a fierce wind howled through the forest and over the camps, spreading alarm everywhere. A fearful storm soon broke upon us in all its fury. Vivid flashes of lightning vaulted along the clouds, filled the heavens with the glare of light, then coursed along our batteries from one end of the line to the other until the scene became one grand and sublime picture. Now the lightning has killed two men in a shelter tent; now a battery has been struck and a gun carriage shattered...Then the thunder crashed and rolled fiercely; the animals started and pricked up their ears at each flash of lightning; and the roar and violence of the storm increased until the very heavens seemed to be rending asunder. I had witnessed thunder storms in the tropics, but none of them compared to this. A captain of the British army who accompanied General McClellan during the campaign and had been several years in India declared he had seen nothing so violent as this storm.

"When night set in, the rain fell like a deluge...accompanied by this violent thunder and lightning...Trees were uprooted, tents blown down, the bridges over the Chickahominy nearly swept away, and the very earth flooded."[40]

Keyes recalled: "Throughout all the night of the 30th of May there was raging a storm the like of which I cannot remember. Torrents of rain drenched the earth, the thunder bolts rolled and fell without intermission, and the heavens flashed with a perpetual blaze of lightning."[41]

Another Union officer recalled that the lightning came in "sheets of flame which enveloped whole bivouacs in eerie glow" and described an "electric fire" that ran along the stacked muskets, "tipping the points of the bayonets with flame, like jets of gas..."[42] This was almost certainly an observation of St. Elmo's fire, a continuous electrical discharge sometimes seen around pointed objects when violent weather creates strong electrical fields near the ground.

E. P. Alexander described the weather as "...a violent rain-storm, scarcely second to any in violence, according to my recollection, that I saw during the war."[43]

Clearly, this was no ordinary storm. The unusual conditions in the atmosphere appear to have continued into May 31. In the words of Adams: "Saturday morning, the 31st, was dull and wet. The storm had

ceased, but the roads were flooded, the woods were weeping, and a
pale gray mist hung over...." At about 9:00 A.M., he states that "...the
fleecy fog began to lift and roll away toward the west, and the houses
on the opposite hills took a more distinct and clear outline."[44]

Other sources seem to confirm that the thirty-first started foggy
and then started to clear.[45] The presence of fog would indicate the likelihood of a temperature inversion, whose refractive effects might have
been responsible for the ability of those in Richmond to hear the battle.
But Adams's statement offers another possible culprit. The typical
weather system in central Virginia tends to move from west to east, yet
Adams saw the fog carried off to the west.

This clearing might indicate an incoming high-pressure system
pushing off the storm to the east. This type of fair weather system would
have an anticyclonic, or clockwise) airflow. Depending on one's position relative to this circular flow, this might have the effect of carrying
water vapor off to the west.

Other reports indicate that, though things had settled down on the
ground, the winds aloft were still forceful. Though Union balloonist
Thaddeus Lowe was able to make some important observations later
in the day, but until 2:00 p.m. he declared the winds too violent to
ascend.[46]

What would such a high-pressure system have meant at Johnston's
location? If one imagines Old Tavern at twelve o'clock on a clock face
and Seven Pines at three o'clock, then a clockwise air flow would have
put Johnston directly upwind from the battle. This, as described in chapter 2, would be the worst place to be for hearing the sounds of the
fighting. A line in Smith's report may confirm this wind direction, as
he talks about conditions around 10:00 A.M.: "During these delays the
firing of cannon across the Chickahominy, and reports from our troops
guarding the river between New Bridge and Mechanicsville, indicated
threatening movements of the Federals on that side."[47] The cannons to
which he refers could possibly be those of Sumner to the northeast, but
are more likely those of Porter or Franklin to the northwest. If the wind
circulation was as described above, Johnston and Smith would have
been downwind (and thus in a region of enhanced audibility) from these
guns.

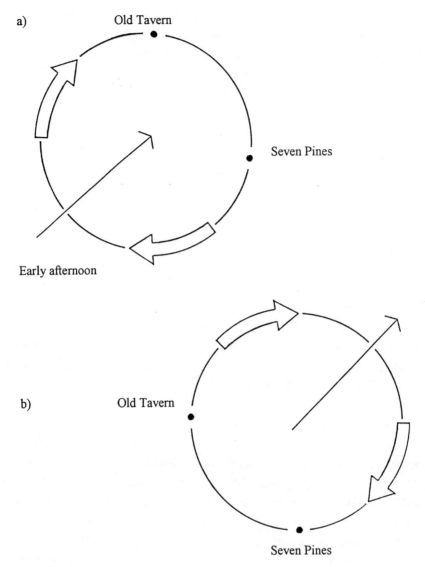

a) Old Tavern

Seven Pines

Early afternoon

b) Old Tavern

Seven Pines

Late afternoon

Fig. 5.6. Possible Scenario for Unusual Acoustics at Seven Pines

(a) Counterclockwise flow of air causes Johnston's headquarters at Fair Oaks to be upwind from Seven Pines; (b) As front moves through, Johnston is now downwind from the battle—sounds become audible.

John M. Early

If the front moved through from southwest to northeast, Johnston would eventually have found himself downwind from the battle (now picturing Seven Pines at six o'clock on the clock face and Old Tavern at nine o'clock) and thus able to hear it. In at least one version of the battle, this is exactly what happened.

Sometime between 2:30 and 3:00 P.M. the frustrated Johnston sent Major Jasper Whiting (Smith's chief of staff) off to the Williamsburg Road to find out what was happening. Whiting returned around 4:00 P.M., apparently with a note from Longstreet informing Johnston that the battle was on and the Confederates were winning but hard-pressed. If Johnston sent in reinforcements right away they might still carry the day.

In a letter to Smith, dated June 28, 1862, Johnston wrote: "Just before 4 o'clock we heard musketry for the first time, and Whiting (General) was ordered to advance. Just then Major W. rode up and reported from L." If indeed the firing suddenly became audible around 4:00 P.M. at Old Tavern, it would support the type of weather scenario described above. None of the official reports indicate that the battle itself was any more intense at that time than earlier.

In his official report, Smith also states that "Between 4 and 5 o'clock heavy musketry was distinctly heard."[48] Douglas Freeman states (without attribution) that the previously muffled sounds "swelled at 4 o'clock into furious small-arms fire."[49] Of course, it is possible that both Smith and Johnston suddenly found the musketry "magically" audible after being informed by Jasper Whiting that the battle was actually already on.

Johnston finally took action around 4:00 P.M. The acoustics and Longstreet's note probably played a part, as did the arrival during the afternoon of several high-level observers, including General Robert E. Lee and President Jefferson Davis. Also present was Gustavus W. Smith, Johnston's second in command. Author Steven Newton makes a good case for there being a great deal of tension between Johnston and Smith.[50] Johnston apparently did not want to share any of the glory of a victory with Smith (and also did not trust his abilities) and had assigned him to command the left wing of the Confederate forces. These forces were not likely to be directly involved in the attack on Seven Pines.

Smith, however, dismissed the idea and proclaimed A. P. Hill able to control the left wing and also decided that it would not be "fair" to take back control of his division now that it had been given to Whiting. This left him free to look over Johnston's shoulder during the course of the day and later report all that he saw. It is through Smith that we learn of Johnston's original plan, with Longstreet attacking down the Nine Mile Road. Johnston and Longstreet do not mention this original plan in their reports. To do so would certainly have not made either man look good in light of subsequent events.

After receiving Longstreet's note, Johnston realized that an immediate attack down the Nine Mile Road was the Confederate's only hope for salvaging the day. Three of Smith's (Whiting's) brigades were in the vicinity of Old Tavern (under three men who would prove themselves good fighters in future battles: John Bell Hood, James J. Pettigrew, and William Dorsey Pender) and it is with these men that Johnston tried to set things right.

Johnston set Hood's men off with orders to keep the Nine Mile Road to their left and to connect with Hill's left flank extending north from the Williamsburg Road.[51] This brigade got lost in the woods for most of the rest of the day. Pettigrew's and Pender's men marched east also, with Pender's men keeping their right flank on the Nine Mile Road. A couple of hours earlier, these men would have had a great effect on the battle at Seven Pines. Now it was too late. Unknown to Johnston, Union troops under Sumner had managed to work their way across the Chickahominy below the point where Whiting's other two brigades were keeping watch. As the Confederates under Pettigrew and Pender marched toward Seven Pines, Sumner's troops were marching directly toward their left flank.

The going was tough due to the thick foliage, but the two Confederate brigades pushed onward until stopped by a valiant defense by two Union regiments just north of Fair Oaks station. The 65th New York and the 1st Minnesota had been at the far right of Keyes's line and had become separated from the fighting at Seven Pines. As the Confederates prepared to break these two Union regiments with another assault, they were stunned to be hit in the flank by the first of Sumner's men.

The fight at Fair Oaks grew in intensity and continued until darkness ended the issue as a draw. After the fight began north of the Nine

Mile Road, Johnston had continued riding down the road, apparently looking for Hood and Longstreet. The addition of Hood's men to the Confederate forces north of the road might have made the difference, but Johnston (apparently discounting the possibility that any sizable force could have crossed the river) directed Hood to continue hunting for Hill's left. He apparently was then able to clearly hear firing from Hill's left flank to the southwest.[52]

As Johnston and his staff hurried back toward the scene of the fighting at Fair Oaks, he held out hope that the fight could be renewed in the morning, and gave orders for each regiment to sleep where it stood. Just then (about 7:30 P.M.) Johnston was struck in the shoulder by a musket ball and a moment later by a shell fragment that unhorsed him.[53] Johnston was seriously injured and was carried first to a house along the roadside and then in an ambulance to Richmond.[54]

The Aftermath

After Johnston had been shot, his command fell to Major General Smith. At this time, Smith was lying on a couch in a farmhouse near the Nine Mile Road, apparently overcome with an anxiety attack.[55] With some difficulty, he was located and brought to Jefferson Davis. Davis asked Smith what he planned to do next and Smith told him, in essence, that he didn't have a clue. Not surprisingly, "Mr. Davis did not seem pleased with what I said," according to Smith.[56]

Smith eventually met with Longstreet late during that night and they decided to resume the attack the next morning. They could not agree on the method, though, as each wanted the other's forces to begin the attack. Finally, Smith ordered Longstreet to attack with his men as soon after daybreak as possible.

Once again, Longstreet failed to carry out his orders. He met with Major General Daniel H. Hill and gave him command of most of Longstreet's division. When Hill asked for his instructions, Longstreet said cryptically, "You have taken the bull by the horns and must fight him out," and then rode off for the rest of the morning.[57]

Hill did launch a small attack on the Union position early on June 1, but his weary men were unable to make much progress and the fighting was inconclusive. By noon on that day, the battle of Seven Pines ended. At about 1:30 P.M., Davis returned to Smith's headquarters and asked if Smith had seen General Robert E. Lee. When Smith asked why Davis wanted Lee, Davis informed him that he had instructed Lee to assume command of Johnston's army. Within a month, Lee would launch an attack on McClellan's right wing at Mechanicsville that would eventually drive the Union army all the way back to Maryland.

It would be almost a year before Johnston would be able to take the field again. Newton makes a convincing argument that Johnston's loss of control at Seven Pines was instrumental in preventing him from fighting any but defensive battles for the rest of the war.[58] Only at Bentonville, North Carolina, near the war's end, did Johnston take to the offensive again, and once again only out of desperation.

There is little doubt that if the acoustic shadow had not prevented Johnston from ordering a timely attack down the Nine Mile Road, the Confederates would have won the battle of Seven Pines. In the words of Douglas Freeman: "Good staff work and prompt reports would have offset failure to hear the sound of battle. Lacking notice from Longstreet, the 'acoustic shadow,' which disguised the rattle of Hill's muskets, was the chief reason for the late launching of the attack by the Confederate left."[59]

From the Union perspective, in the words of Major General Keyes: "The left of my line was all protected by the White Oak Swamp, but the right was on ground so favorable to the approach of the enemy, and so far from the Chickahominy, that if Johnston had attacked there an hour or two earlier than he did, I could have made but a feeble defense comparatively, and every man of us would have been killed, captured or driven into the swamp or river before assistance could have reached us."[60]

One can certainly make the case that the acoustic shadow that placed Joseph Johnston in the wrong place at the wrong time was a key element in Robert E. Lee's rise to fame. It's possible, as will be discussed in the final chapter of this book, that another acoustic shadow began the final act of Lee's military career.

Chapter 6

Iuka, Mississippi

An ill wind would blow away from Ulysses S. Grant once again, this time at Iuka, Mississippi. He would not be as lucky here as at Fort Donelson.

Background

After the capture of Forts Henry and Donelson, there was a temporary halt to Union progress in the West. Though Ulysses S. Grant wanted to push south, Henry Halleck ordered him to hold his position. This was ostensibly so that forces under Don Carlos Buell (now a major general), commander of the Department of the Ohio, could join up with Grant. It was really more of a political maneuver by Halleck, who had become jealous of Grant's success and growing reputation.

In his desire for overall command in the western theater, Halleck at first saw Buell as his main rival. Grant's successes along the Cumberland and Tennessee Rivers and the subsequent fawning over him by the national press had now brought him into the picture.

Shortly after the victory at Fort Donelson, Buell moved south and took Nashville. Without asking Halleck's permission, Grant traveled to Nashville to meet with Buell.[1] The meeting angered Halleck to the point that he began a smear campaign against Grant. He wrote to Union General in Chief George B. McClellan that Grant had "left his command without my authority….It is hard to censure a successful general immediately after a victory, but I think he richly deserves it. I can get no returns, no reports, no information of any kind from him…I am worn out and tired with this neglect and inefficiency." Halleck also hinted that Grant was living up to his reputation as a hard drinker: "A rumor has just reached me that since the taking of Fort Donelson General Grant has resumed his former bad habits. If so, it will account for his neglect of my often-repeated orders."

McClellan agreed to let Halleck replace Grant with his subordinate Charles F. Smith. This caused such an uproar among Grant's field officers and also among Grant's supporters in Washington that Abraham Lincoln stepped in and ordered Grant reinstated. Grant was not only reinstated, but also promoted to major general. To stabilize the situation in the West and to mollify Halleck, Halleck was given overall command over both Grant and Buell.

After the defeats at Forts Henry and Donelson, Confederate General Albert Sidney Johnston had made the unpopular, but correct, decision to evacuate central and western Tennessee. He dropped back to the crucial railroad intersection of Corinth, Mississippi. Here the Memphis and Charleston Railroad running east-west crossed the Mobile and Ohio Railroad running north-south. The former was especially important as it was the only direct link in the Confederacy between the East Coast and the Mississippi River. At Corinth, Johnston's army joined up with forces under General Pierre G. T. Beauregard.

Grant moved his forces down the Tennessee River to camp at Pittsburg Landing, about 20 miles northeast of Corinth, to wait for Buell's army. From there, Halleck planned to assault the Confederates at Corinth. Johnston moved first, though, and attacked the unsuspecting Grant on April 5, 1862. The Union army was being pushed into the river before Grant, not even on the field at the beginning of the fight, managed to avert disaster. By April 7, the Confederates had retreated back to Corinth. The popular Johnston was killed in what came to be called the battle of Shiloh (in honor of a prominent church on the battlefield).

Despite the near disaster, Halleck was still focusing on Corinth as an important strategic objective. To ensure a successful assault on the town, he gathered one hundred twenty-five thousand men in three armies at Pittsburg Landing.[2] These included Grant's army, the Army of the Ohio under Buell, and the Army of the Mississippi under Major General John Pope. The latter force had successfully cleared the upper Mississippi River stronghold Island Number 10.

The Confederates had constructed a strong series of earthworks around Corinth, but Beauregard (now in command) realized that the position was untenable in the face of Halleck's numbers. In late May, the Confederates withdrew 52 miles farther south down the Mobile and Ohio Railroad to Tupelo.[3] With part of his force, Halleck then seized the nearly empty town of Corinth. By the first week of June, his entire base of operations had been shifted there.

On June 16, the now ill Beauregard left for Mobile and transferred his command temporarily to General Braxton Bragg. Confederate President Jefferson Davis, who disliked Beauregard, used this unauthorized absence as an excuse to place Bragg in permanent command. By abandoning Corinth, the Confederates had given up any hope of reinforcing the small force guarding Memphis. On June 6, Union forces took Memphis; the Mississippi River was now clear to Vicksburg, Mississippi.

An aggressive general might now have pushed his advantage, but Halleck was cautious. He spread his men westward across the Memphis and Charleston Railroad to repair and guard the tracks from guerilla forces. Following wishes by his superiors in Washington to take eastern Tennessee, whose population was highly sympathetic to the Union, Halleck sent Buell and 30,000 men off towards Chattanooga.

The Union command situation at Corinth changed drastically over the next two months. Both Pope and Halleck were called to Washington, Pope to lead Union forces in Virginia (where he would soon be humiliated at the battle of Second Manassas), and Halleck to replace McClellan as general in chief of the Union armies. This left Grant in command of just over 60,000 men in the Army of Tennessee and the Army of the Mississippi. Buell's Army of the Ohio, marching on Chattanooga, was outside his command.

In late July, Bragg decided to make a move. It was not to be in northern Mississippi, however. He informed Richmond that he was moving much of his force to Chattanooga, both to help in its defense, and also to use the area as a staging ground from which to attack either central Tennessee or into Kentucky. Bragg organized the department he was abandoning into three districts: the District of the Gulf, under Brigadier General John H. Forney and based in Mobile; the District of the Mississippi, under Major General Earl Van Dorn, based in Vicksburg; and the District of the Tennessee, under Major General Sterling Price, based at Tupelo.

Bragg left Price with vague instructions to keep Grant from reinforcing Buell and to hold the remaining length of the Mobile and Ohio Railroad that was under Confederate control. On August 2, however, Bragg mistakenly informed Price that most of the Union army had moved with Buell towards Chattanooga and that Price now had an opportunity to attack through Corinth and into western Tennessee.[4] Price, not giving full credence to Bragg's reports, did not want to proceed north without support from Van Dorn. Van Dorn, however, was preoccupied with matters closer to the Mississippi River, and responded by asking Price to give him some of his men.

Meanwhile, the Union War Department was siphoning more men from Grant to help Buell. By early September, Grant had at Corinth only two divisions under Major General William S. Rosecrans. Bragg now had Buell on the run towards Nashville, and on September 2, Bragg sent a telegram to Price ordering him to prevent Rosecrans from joining Buell or to follow him closely if he escaped Corinth.[5] Price decided he must attack Rosecrans, even without Van Dorn's help.

Rosecrans had dispersed some of his force south of Corinth to shield the position. The most reliable supply route for his men was the Tennessee River (because of guerilla attacks on the railroads), and Rosecrans placed a brigade at Iuka to protect the river landings. It was toward Iuka that Price headed on September 11. At this point, Price was under the impression that most of Rosecrans's force would be at Iuka, preparing for a departure north across the Tennessee River to join Buell. Grant and Rosecrans were expecting an attack, but they thought that it would come at Corinth. Accordingly, most of the Rosecrans's men were concentrated there.

Iuka was a nice little town, known across the nation for its mineral springs. Four roads (as well as the Memphis and Charleston Railroad) came into Iuka. The Eastport and Fulton Stage Route came in from the northeast and the Iuka and Corinth Stage Route came in from the west. The Jacinto Road and the Fulton Road came in from the south.

On the morning of September 13, Confederate cavalry under Brigadier General Frank C. Armstrong arrived at Iuka. They quickly overwhelmed the Union pickets before being driven back by the main Union force. The Union leader, Colonel Robert Murphy, had been charged by Rosecrans with the defense of Iuka until the substantial stores (30 carloads) there could be removed. He waited throughout the day for a train to arrive to take the supplies to Corinth. The telegraph line (and the railroad track between Burnsville and Iuka) to Corinth had been cut, and several couriers sent by Murphy did not reach their destination.[6]

Finally, early on the morning of September 14, Murphy decided he could wait no longer. He ordered Iuka evacuated and detailed a company of cavalry to burn the supplies. When Confederate cavalry entered the town at 7:00 A.M., the supplies had still not been burned; as a result they fell into the hands of the hungry Southern troops. Grant was disgusted at Murphy's feeble resistance, so Grant later had him brought up on court-martial charges.[7]

At this point, both sides were confused about the other's intentions. Grant and Rosecrans could make little sense of Price's occupation of Iuka. They reasoned that it must be either a precursor to a movement across the Tennessee River to join Bragg or a preliminary diversion before a simultaneous attack on Corinth with Van Dorn's forces.

Price had gone to Iuka expecting to meet Rosecrans's full force there and was surprised to find that he had retreated to Corinth. He decided that his best move now was to hold Rosecrans where he was (to prevent him aiding Buell) and to petition Van Dorn once again to make a joint attack on Corinth. He sent couriers to Van Dorn on the fourteenth bearing this request.[8]

Grant, always aggressive, decided that regardless of Price's intentions, now was the time to go after him. His information indicated that Van Dorn was at least four days from Corinth, thus he could not aid Price. On September 16, Grant formulated a plan: a force of eight thousand men under Major General Edward O. Ord would move on Price from Burnsville, about seven miles to the northwest of Iuka, while nine thousand men commanded by Rosecrans simultaneously attacked Price from the south. Enough men would be left at Rienzi and Jacinto to prevent a surprise attack on Corinth. All troops were to be in position on the night of September 18, and Ord was to begin the battle the next morning.

Fig. 6.1. Edward Ord

Library of Congress

**Fig. 6.2.
William Rosecrans**

Library of Congress

Fig. 6.3. Sterling Price (*center*)

This photograph of Price and other Confederate generals was taken in Mexico after the war.

Fig. 6.4. Northern Mississippi and Western Tennessee

Battles and Leaders of the Civil War

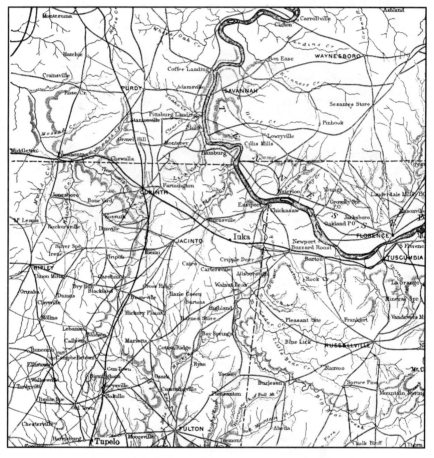

Fig. 6.5. The Corinth and Iuka Region

Battles and Leaders of the Civil War

The Battle and the Acoustics

In Grant's original plan, both Ord and Rosecrans would move on Iuka along the path of the Memphis and Charleston Railroad, with Ord to the north of the tracks and Rosecrans to the south. Rosecrans suggested that since many of his men were already at Jacinto, it might be better to have them attack Price from the south and southwest. They were already in position to do so, and the land between Jacinto (14 miles west of Iuka)[9] and Iuka was better than that between Burnsville and Iuka. If Ord and Rosecrans attacked together, Price would be trapped. Rosecrans would send his men against Price along both of the roads that entered Iuka from the south, the Jacinto Road and the Fulton Road.

To successfully execute a pincer movement, such as the one proposed, was difficult, even on good terrain, which this was not. Since Price's army was bigger (approximately 11,000 men) than either jaw of the pincer, the two attacks must begin simultaneously to be successful. Grant assumed that Rosecrans would be close enough to Iuka by late on the eighteenth that the attack could begin at 4:30 A.M. on the nineteenth.

A heavy rainstorm on September 17 delayed movement of those of Rosecrans's troops still in Corinth attempting to join those already in Jacinto. Rosecrans sent a message to Grant that he would not have his men together at Jacinto until 2:00 P.M. on the nineteenth. This turned out to be optimistic. Rosecrans's division under Brigadier General David S. Stanley was misled by a guide into heading towards Burnsville and did not arrive at Jacinto until late on the eighteenth. Rosecrans sent a dispatch to Grant:

> Headquarters Encampment, *September* 18, 1862
>
> GENERAL: Your dispatch received. General Stanley's division arrived after dark, having been detained by falling in the rear of Ross through fault of guide. Our cavalry 6 miles this side of Barnett's; Hamilton's First Brigade 8 miles, Second Brigade 9 miles this side; Stanley's near Davenport's Mill. We shall move as early as practicable, by 4:30 a.m. This will give 20 miles' march for Stanley to Iuka. Shall not therefore be there before 1 or 2 o'clock, but when we come in will endeavor to do it strongly.
>
> W. S. ROSECRANS
>
> *Brigadier-General, U.S. Army*[10]

This dispatch disappointed Grant, as he expected that by late on the eighteenth Rosecrans would be well on the way to Iuka.[11] He decided to alter the method by which the simultaneous pincer attack would be made. Instead of setting a time for the attack, he showed Ord the dispatch from Rosecrans, and told Ord to drive in the Confederate pickets but *not bring on an engagement until he heard the sounds of Rosecrans attacking from the south.* The courier was sent back to Rosecrans with this change in plans.

No copy of the dispatch bearing these instructions to Ord has survived. In his official report, Grant indicates that the order to wait for the sounds of Rosecrans's guns was sent to Ord along with the copy of Rosecrans's dispatch.[12] Ord indicates in his report that he received the notification that Rosecrans was behind schedule at about 10:00 A.M. on the nineteenth:

> September 19, 1862
>
> GENERAL: I send you dispatch received from Rosecrans late in the night. You will see that he is behind where we expected him. Do not be too rapid with your advance this morning, unless it should be found that the enemy are evacuating. By order of Major-General Grant:
>
> Clark. B. Lagow
> *Colonel and Inspector-General*[13]

This message does not mention the proposed acoustic signal, so it is possible that those directions were sent verbally with the courier. It is also possible that Grant was confused about when the order to wait on Rosecrans's guns was given. Ord states that Grant gave him this order at about 4:00 P.M. on the nineteenth, when he had returned to Grant's headquarters to consult with him. In his report, Grant also states that he gave (or repeated) the order to Ord at that time.

Neither Ord nor Grant give any explanation for why Ord did not begin his attack at 4:30 A.M. as previously ordered. If Ord did not receive word of Rosecrans's delay until 10:00 A.M., he was disobeying orders by not making his attack as planned. It is also hard to understand why the message took so long to get to Ord. Grant states that Rosecrans's message arrived at his headquarters "after midnight." At the time, Ord was about six miles from Iuka and Grant was at Burnsville, just a bit farther up the railroad; they couldn't have been separated by more than two or three miles.

In any event, Ord's men spent the nineteenth in minor skirmishes with the Confederate pickets northeast of Iuka. Rosecrans's men, however, were marching rapidly toward Iuka. Rosecrans directed Stanley to take his men up the Jacinto Road while another division under Brigadier General Charles S. Hamilton came up on Price along the Fulton Road.

When Rosecrans arrived at Barnett's Crossroads, where the paths of his two forces would split, he realized a major fault in his plan. The two roads, which he thought to be separated by a couple of miles, were actually about five miles apart. The intervening land, like most of the area around Iuka, was impassable. It consisted of hills and deep ravines covered with dense trees and shrubs, with an occasional swamp thrown in. With no way to communicate between the two columns, Price could destroy either force individually. Rosecrans decided to send all his men up the Jacinto Road to Iuka. In this he made another serious error by leaving the Fulton Road open as an escape route for Price.

As the first of his troops headed up the Jacinto Road, it was about 1:00 P.M., only an hour before the time Rosecrans had told Grant he would be at Iuka. He was still about eight miles away.[14] Shortly after heading up the Jacinto Road, Rosecrans's men began to run into Confederate cavalry, slowly pushing them back towards Iuka. About four miles from Iuka, the Confederate cavalry dismounted and put up a stiffer resistance near a house owned by the Moore family of Iuka.[15] Pushing the cavalry back once more, the Union troops angrily set fire to the house sometime between 2:00 P.M. and 3:00 P.M.[16] The lead elements of Rosecrans's forces came upon the main Confederate force two miles farther up the road and now two miles from Iuka. It was now about 4:30 P.M.

Early on the morning of the nineteenth, Price had heard from Van Dorn. He had finally assented to a joint attack on Corinth and requested that Price and his army join forces with him at Rienzi. The dispatch also informed Price that Jefferson Davis had granted Van Dorn rank over him whenever the two should join forces. At this point, Price was happy to have some direct course of action to follow and replied that he would march toward Rienzi the next morning.[17]

Also on this morning, Price received a strange message from the Federals, informing him that he should lay down his arms as the war was all but over: the Army of Northern Virginia under General Robert E. Lee had been routed and destroyed at the battle of Antietam in Maryland. This misinformation had been sent in a telegram from Washington to Grant's headquarters, where it was passed along in good faith to Price. Price paid it no mind.[18]

Price was completely shocked by the news of Rosecrans's forces coming up the Jacinto Road. He had been expecting an attack from the direction of Burnsville for two days and except for the cavalry pickets he had no one between Rosecrans and Iuka. When he received word at about 2:30 P.M. of Rosecrans's advance, Price immediately shifted his attention southward, and gave orders for several brigades to move quickly to the Jacinto Road. Shortly after 4:00 P.M., Price had 18 regiments and two batteries hurried into position to face 17 regiments and six batteries for the Federals.[19]

The steep hills and heavily wooded terrain made it hard for the soldiers, many facing battle for the first time, to get into position. Nevertheless, by 4:30 P.M. a sharp and vicious battle had begun. The Confederates repeatedly charged a Union battery perched high on one of the hills, with a good many of the attackers and artillerists dying on the point of a bayonet. In Rosecrans's official report he describes the action:

> The battle became furious. Our battery poured in a deadly fire upon the enemy's column advancing up the road, while their musketry, concentrated upon it, soon killed or wounded most of our horses....The roar of musketry was terrific.[20]

Many of the subordinate officers mentioned the severity of both the musketry and the artillery fire during the course of the battle.[21] The soldiers fought back and forth over a ridge until almost 8:00 P.M., when the Union troops finally conceded the ridge to the exhausted Confederates. The battle of Iuka was essentially a draw, though both sides later claimed victory.

But what had happened to Ord? Early on the afternoon of the nineteenth, Price had his entire force facing to the northeast, expecting an attack from Ord. When he recovered from the shock of learning of

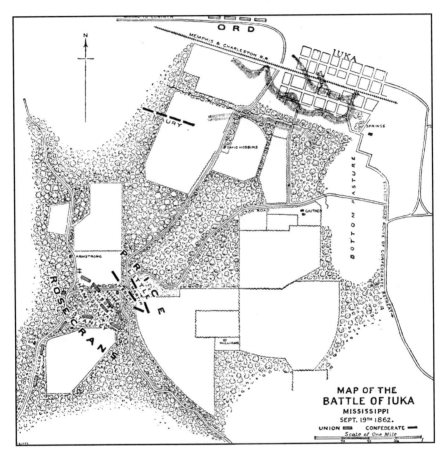

Fig. 6.6. The Battle of Iuka

Battles and Leaders of the Civil War

Rosecrans's approach from the southwest, he shifted most of his men to the Jacinto Road, leaving Ord almost unopposed. An attack from Ord at any time would have certainly been disaster for the Confederates.

By 4:00 P.M. on the nineteenth, Ord had certainly received the order from Grant to attack at the first sounds of battle from Rosecrans's direction. Sometime shortly thereafter, Ord issued the order throughout his command. At about 6:00 P.M., Ord received the following dispatch from Brigadier General Leonard F. Ross:

> September 19, 1862–4 p.m.
>
> Major-General ORD:
>
> For the last twenty minutes there has been a dense smoke arising from the direction of Iuka. I conclude that the enemy are evacuating and destroying the stores.
>
> L.F. ROSS
> Brigadier-General[22]

Several reports of the battle mention the dense smoke associated with the fighting: "The smoke soon became so dense that we could scarcely see the man next to us..."[23]; "The smoke hung over the battlefield like a cloud, obscuring every object ten feet off."[24]

Still, if the time of Ross's dispatch is correct, the heavy smoke rising from the direction of Iuka can hardly have been from the fighting, which did not begin in earnest until 4:30 P.M. The smoke most certainly was rising from the burning Moore house.

It is very odd that neither Ord nor Ross would send a reconnaissance party to investigate the smoke. Whether the smoke was coming from Price burning stores, as Ross suggested, or from fighting, an alert and aggressive commander would surely have wanted to investigate. Still, with Price nearly withdrawn from his front, Ord did nothing as he waited in vain for sounds of battle.

It was not until the morning of September 20 that Ord finally moved. As we will see, he claimed that, in accordance with Grant's orders, he did not move until he heard the sounds of firing. Grant at Burnsville also appears to have been bathed in silence. In his report he claims that he first became aware of Rosecrans's fight when he received the following dispatch at 8:35 A.M. on the twentieth:

HDQRS. ARMY OF THE MISSISSIPI, TWO MILES SOUTH
OF IUKA, MISS.,

September 19, 1862–10:30 p.m.

GENERAL: We met the enemy in force just above this point. The engagement lasted several hours. We have lost two or three pieces of artillery. Firing was very heavy. You must attack in the morning and in force. The ground is horrid, unknown to us, and no room for development. Could not use our artillery at all. Fired but few shots. Push into them until we can have time to do something. We will try to get a position on our right which will take Iuka.

W.S. ROSECRANS

Brigadier-General, U.S. Army[25]

Grant immediately sent the following note to Ord:

BURNSVILLE, *September* 20, 1862–8:35 a.m.

General ORD:

Get your troops up and attack as soon as possible. Rosecrans had two hours' fight last night and now this morning again, and unless you can create a diversion in his favor he may find his hands full. Hurry your troops all possible.

U.S. GRANT

Major-General[26]

In his report, Grant states that the phrase "now this morning again" was based on his hearing firing at Iuka from his position at Burnsville. Ord had also heard the firing on this morning and in accordance with Grant's orders had already moved his men out. Ord states in his report that "the next morning at 8 o'clock, hearing guns in front of us, I moved rapidly into Iuka and found it had been evacuated during the night."[27]

The guns that Ord and Grant heard were from the Union First Missouri artillery, which was shelling the nearly empty town of Iuka. Price had decided by early on the twentieth to make his escape and join Van Dorn. As he states in his report:

I had proposed to renew the battle in the morning and had made my dispositions accordingly, but having ascertained toward morning that the enemy had by means of the two railroads massed against me a greatly superior force, and knowing that my position was such that a battle would endanger the safety of my trains even if I should be victorious, of which I had but little doubt, I determined to adhere to my original purpose and to make the movement upon which I had already agreed with General Van Dorn.[28]

Rousing his men at 3:00 A.M., Price got them headed south on the unguarded Fulton Road. By 8:00 A.M., most of the Confederates had cleared Iuka, and by 2:00 P.M. they were safely eight miles south of town. At dawn, Union skirmishers had advanced on Iuka and shot a few shells into the town, evidently heard by both Grant and Ord. There was a bit of rear guard fighting, but the Confederates had made good their escape.

At 9:45 A.M., Rosecrans sent a dispatch to Grant stating that the Confederates were in full retreat. He concluded the message with the statement: "Why did you not attack this morning?" The message apparently got into the hands of Brigadier General James B. McPherson, who was with Ord. Before passing the note onto Grant, Ord wrote upon it: "We didn't hear any sounds of battle last p.m. Started with sounds of first guns for town."[29]

How could Ord have not heard any sound from a violent battle within five miles of his position? In his official report, Ord offers an answer:

> The guns heard that morning (the 20th, 8 a.m.) were the first heard by us, although on the afternoon of the 19th the head of General Rosecrans's column had engaged the enemy 2 miles south of Iuka about the time that General Ross reported smoke in the direction of Iuka. The wind, freshly blowing from us in the direction of Iuka during the whole of the 19th, prevented our hearing the guns and co-operating with General Rosecrans.[30]

There is likely some truth in Ord's assertion. A rainstorm such as that on the night of September 18, which did not end until about 10:00 A.M. on the day of the battle, would typically be followed by clearing and temporary windy conditions as the system moved off to the east. By the night of the nineteenth and the morning of the twentieth, the wind had died down. This calming would have allowed Ord and Grant to hear the sparse shooting on the morning of the twentieth when they heard nothing of the violent fight.

According to Rosecrans's head surgeon, "The night was calm and without a breath of air stirring, so that, as the battle raged until after nightfall, we were enabled to dress the wounded by candle-light as well as if we had been inside a house."[31] This seems to indicate that the air near the battlefield itself may have been calm during the battle. One Union soldier wrote that "The evening was one of those damp, dull, cloudy ones, which caused the smoke to settle down about as high as a man's head."[32] This would seem to indicate a relatively still atmosphere.

A number of Union soldiers seemed to corroborate Ord's account. In letters and diaries, at least four men noted that they heard nothing of the battle just to their south. One soldier in Ord's command, however, wrote that he had heard the "thunder of cannon" from the direction of Rosecrans's column at about 5:00 P.M. on the nineteenth.[33]

It is not implausible that all these accounts are truthful and accurate. A wind trailing a storm is common and so wind-induced refraction of sound would certainly be possible at upwind sites such as Ord's and Grant's headquarters. In the turbulence of such an atmosphere, it would also not be uncommon for the sound to be unrefracted or even refracted downwards in some spots to the north and northwest of the battle, accounting for some of Ord's soldiers hearing the sounds.

The terrain around the battlefield was not conducive to the propagation of sound or to the movement of air. Some descriptions of the terrain include "the thickest place I ever saw of vines, bushes, and briars"[34]; "The underbrush and timber were too thick to admit of deployments, and the most that could be done was to take a position across the road"[35]; and "thick wood and brush"[36]

With the dense foliage and the steep contours of the land, it is likely that the wind experienced by Ord six miles north was stifled on the Jacinto Road battlefield. It is also plausible that such terrain would prevent much direct sound from propagating in any direction near ground level. Once aloft, the sounds would be subject to upward or downward refraction depending on the direction of propagation.

There was relatively little artillery used during the battle due to the nature of the terrain. The higher frequency sounds of the small arms would be much more susceptible to absorption and interaction with the surrounding foliage.

The Aftermath

Rosecrans apparently never believed Ord's explanation for his lack of action. He wondered how Ord could be in silence when Colonel John Du Bois, 15 miles away "in a straight line over a rolling forest country," reportedly heard the noise distinctly.[37] As explained in chapter 2, it is certainly not impossible for a listener at significant distance from a sound source to hear it when it is inaudible to a listener much closer to the source. It is the opinion of the author that Ord was in an acoustic shadow, and not intentionally trying to avoid a fight.

Grant, who also did not hear Rosecrans's battle until the morning of September 20, seemed to accept Ord's explanation, perhaps more easily after his own experience at Fort Donelson. He was more concerned with Rosecrans's failure to cover the Fulton Road, allowing Price to escape. Having let an outnumbered and cornered foe get away was embarrassing, but Grant tried to make the best of it in his report:

> During the night the enemy fled, leaving our troops in possession of the field, with their dead to bury and wounded to care for. If it was the object of the enemy to make their way to Kentucky, they were defeated in that; if to hold their position until Van Dorn could come up on the southwest of Corinth and make a simultaneous attack, they were defeated in that. Our only defeat was in not capturing the entire army or in destroying it, as I had hoped to do.[38]

After escaping, Price joined his forces with those of Van Dorn and two weeks later they made a ill-conceived joint attack on Corinth. After initial progress, the Confederates were decimated as they tried to assault the well-fortified town, and limped in retreat to the southwest. A week later, Bragg and Buell fought to a draw at Perryville, Kentucky (see chapter 7). This result, in combination with Van Dorn's disaster at Corinth, induced Bragg to retreat which ended the Confederate invasion in the north. Along with the repulse at Antietam, Southern fortunes had turned decidedly for the worse since the summer of 1862.

Within six months, Sterling Price had been transferred to the Trans-Mississippi Department to serve under General Edmund Kirby Smith. Getting close to his Missouri home had long been a wish of Price. On May 7, 1863, Van Dorn was shot and killed by the husband of a woman with whom Van Dorn had apparently been having an affair.

Rosecrans, upset with Grant's inaction at Iuka and what he perceived to be Grant's poor leadership, became furious with Grant after the battle of Corinth. He felt that Grant's report snubbed his contributions in the battle, which had been considerable, and also he was upset that Grant called off his pursuit of Van Dorn's beaten army after the battle. Luckily for both men, President Lincoln appointed Rosecrans to replace Buell as head of the Army of the Ohio, just a month after the battle of Iuka.

Grant, of course, would eventually wear down the Confederates in Mississippi and took the stronghold at Vicksburg on July 4, 1863. By 1864 he was in Virginia, directing the final push against General Robert E. Lee. Near the end of his effort there, as we will see, he finally became the beneficiary of an acoustic shadow.

Chapter 7

Perryville, Kentucky

In October 1862, Union and Confederate forces clashed near Perryville in Kentucky's largest battle of the Civil War. Unusual acoustics almost caused a disaster for Major General Don Carlos Buell's Union army.

Background

While Sterling Price was extricating himself from the pincers of Edward Ord and William Rosecrans near Iuka, a larger struggle was beginning north of Mississippi. Confederate troops under Major General Braxton Bragg and Major General Edmund Kirby Smith were making a move to take back the large portions of Tennessee and Kentucky lost earlier in the year.

In January 1862, the Confederacy had held most of Kentucky, all of Tennessee, and almost the entire length of the Mississippi River. By the summer, Union armies had completely knocked the Confederates out of Kentucky and had moved through Tennessee into northern Mississippi and Alabama. The Mississippi River had been cleared all the way to Vicksburg.

Things were not much better in the East, where McClellan had his army on the doorstep of the Confederate capital. But in late June, Lee began to turn the tide in Virginia. The Seven Days' Battles would send McClellan reeling back to the James River. By August, Lee would be moving north toward Maryland.

Could something similar be done in the middle part of the Confederacy? If so, it would be up to Bragg, who had taken over command of the Army of Mississippi from P.G.T. Beauregard on June 20, 1862.

Bragg's army was at Tupelo, Mississippi (see chapter 6), about 60 miles south of the main Union concentration at Corinth.

The Union forces at Corinth consisted of three armies, the Army of the Ohio (under Don Carlos Buell), the Army of the Tennessee (under Ulysses S. Grant), and the Army of the Mississippi (under William Rosecrans, replacing John Pope after the latter's transfer to Virginia). After occupying Corinth from Beauregard's retreating Confederates, Henry Halleck (in overall command of the Union troops) had to decide where to attack next.

There was little in Mississippi worth occupying. There were few cities, few roads, and the land was not conducive to supporting a major army. Halleck decided that he would strengthen Corinth's defenses so that it could be successfully held by part of his force, and then send the rest of his men on a new mission. In mid-June, he ordered Buell to take his Army of the Ohio and move on Chattanooga. Buell began to move in late June, but exceedingly slowly. The roads were terrible and the railroads were constantly being cut and attacked by guerilla bands.

Chattanooga, in southeastern Tennessee, was an important strategic target. It was a vital link in the Confederate railway system, and capture of the city would open up operations for Union movements into Georgia and South Carolina. More importantly, in some ways, Chattanooga's capture would be a symbolic strike for the pro-Union populace of eastern Tennessee.

Chattanooga was still in Confederate hands, guarded by a small force. Most of the Confederates in eastern Tennessee were in Knoxville, under Major General Edmund Smith. After Buell began to move toward Chattanooga, Bragg was faced with some difficult choices. He could attempt to move on Corinth, which would now be slightly more vulnerable. He could also move on

Fig. 7.1. Don Carlos Buell

Library of Congress

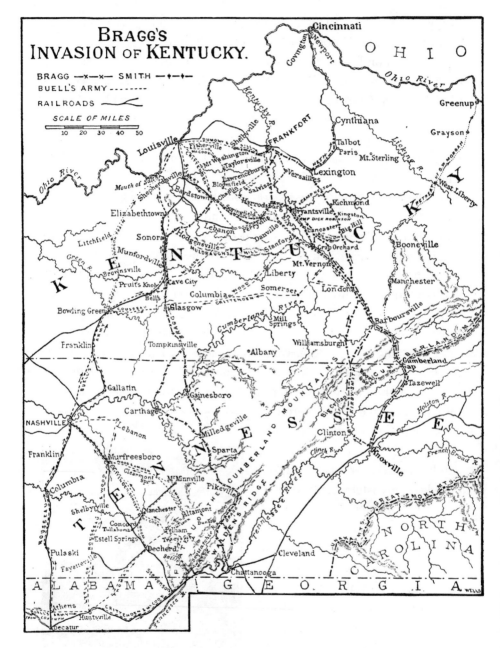

Fig. 7.2. Bragg's Invasion of Kentucky

Battles and Leaders of the Civil War

the rear of Buell's army, but this would have the disadvantage of putting him between Buell and Grant.

Bragg finally decided on a third choice. He would block Buell by getting to Chattanooga first. At the speed that Buell was moving, it was possible. Once there and Chattanooga was made safe, he and Smith could go on the offensive, heading into the middle part of Tennessee and even into Kentucky. Such a threat would surely force much of the Union army to withdraw to the north.

Fig. 7.3. Braxton Bragg

Library of Congress

Such an invasion, along with Lee's push into Maryland, might also be enough to finally earn European recognition or support for the Confederacy. While making his move, Bragg would leave about 16,000 men under Price at Tupelo to keep Grant from reinforcing Buell (this arrangement would lead in September to the battle of Iuka described in chapter 6).

In late July, Bragg finally got his men on the move. In a complicated series of maneuvers, he was able to move more than 30,000 men more than eight hundred miles in six days. The trip took place over six different railroads with six different gauges. By July 29, the first units were arriving in Chattanooga.[1] Two days later, Smith arrived by train from his Knoxville headquarters to discuss future operations with Bragg. It was then that Bragg learned some news that would later be crucial in the upcoming campaign.

Bragg was informed that Smith had an independent command, and he was answerable only to Jefferson Davis. If Bragg and Smith joined their forces, Bragg would take command, but until then Smith could do as he wish. Though Bragg seemed to come away from the meeting with little apprehension about Smith's motives, later events showed that Smith was reluctant to relinquish his authority. Through

Fig. 7.4.
Edmund Kirby Smith

Miller, *The Photographic History of the Civil War*

the next two months, Smith took pains to avoid bringing his forces together with Bragg's.

Initially, Bragg focused on taking back middle Tennessee, especially Nashville. But eventually he and Smith became fixated on Kentucky. Kentucky's political situation was complicated. The populace was almost evenly divided between pro-Union and pro-Confederate sentiments. Many of those in favor of secession lived in the wealthy and fertile lands of the Bluegrass Region in eastern Kentucky. Bragg, Smith, and Jefferson Davis all believed that if Confederate armies rolled back into Kentucky, many men would jump at the opportunity to join their ranks.

Smith made the first move. On August 12, his men began to pull out of Knoxville, heading in three columns toward the Cumberland Mountains. The best passage through the mountains was at Cumberland Gap, but Union forces under Brigadier General George W. Morgan held that route. Smith who briefly toyed with the idea of laying siege to Morgan's force decided the plan impractical. Morgan's defenses were strong, he had plenty of provisions and had 10,000 men, more than half the number Smith commanded. In the end, Smith set about nine thousand men under Brigadier General Carter L. Stevenson to keep Morgan in place, while taking the remainder of his men through other gaps farther south.

Smith headed north through the mountains with about nine thousand infantrymen and nine hundred cavalry troopers. It was an awful journey, with steep hills and little water due to an ongoing drought. But by August 29, Smith and his men had made it over the mountains and into Kentucky, reaching Barboursville on that day.

When word spread that Confederates had entered Kentucky in force, there was near panic in that state and neighboring Ohio. Smith could threaten Louisville and even Cincinnati. Louisville was the northern end of the railroad line supplying Grant and Buell. When informed that Bragg had moved to Chattanooga, the alarmed Buell had detached Major General William Nelson from his command in order to take charge of the defense of Louisville. The citizens of Cincinnati began to frantically build fortifications.

Nelson's first move, after he arrived, was to head to Richmond, about 25 miles south of Lexington. About six thousand green troops were there, under the command of Brigadier General Mahlon Manson and Brigadier General Charles Cruft, and directly in the path of Smith's advancing army. Nelson reached Richmond on August 26 informing Manson and Cruft that he would like to move the men to Danville, about 30 miles to the southwest. Nelson told Manson and Cruft to prepare their men for the move; then he rode back to his headquarters in Lexington.

Before Manson and Cruft could move their men, Smith's Confederates were upon them. On the morning of August 30, the Southerners attacked. At first the untested Yankees put up a stiff fight, but by afternoon Smith had gotten men on each flank of the Union position. Nelson, having received word of the battle, rode hard to Richmond, only to find the Union troops fleeing in a complete rout. He tried to stem the tide. Unfortunately, he was shot in the stomach and captured. By evening on the thirtieth, beaten Federal soldiers were straggling into Lexington.

Proportionally, it was one of the worst Union losses of the war. Of the sixty-five hundred Union soldiers in the fight, more than five thousand were killed, wounded, missing, or captured. In the words of Major General Horatio G. Wright, in command of the Union Department of the Ohio: "The force engaged in the battle in front of Richmond was utterly broken up, and after all the exertions that could be made to collect the stragglers, only some 800 or 900 could be found. The remainder of the force were killed, captured or scattered over the country."[2]

The battle at Richmond essentially cleared the way for Smith throughout the Bluegrass. Wright decided to order all Union forces back to Louisville to protect that city and the rail lines south. Cincinnati was seen as less vulnerable as it was on the north bank of the Ohio River. Smith and his men entered Lexington on September 2, and found the reception to be warm. The citizens of Lexington showed genuine happiness at the Confederate presence, but few were eager to join Smith's army.

At this point, Smith had no knowledge of the whereabouts of either Bragg or Buell. He decided to play the game cautiously now, holding tight at Lexington and waiting for the other armies to show their hand. He sent some units to neighboring towns as a buffer around his main force and even sent a small force north to annoy Cincinnati. But for the most part, he and his men rested and gathered equipment, food, and supplies from the abundant fruits of the countryside. When word reached the Confederates of General Lee's victory at Manassas and subsequent penetration of Maryland, things looked bright.

While Smith was making his way to Lexington, Bragg had finally gotten his men into motion from Chattanooga on August 28. Neither Bragg nor Buell was sure at this point which way Bragg would go. Assuming that Bragg's objective would be Nashville, on August 30 (as Smith was routing the Union forces at Richmond) Buell ordered his forces to concentrate at Murfreesboro, Tennessee. Many later criticized Buell for not making a stand at the base of the Cumberland Mountains. By moving back to Murfreesboro, he had allowed Buell free reign to maneuver in almost any direction.

Once into the lowlands, Bragg decided to bypass Nashville and quickly move north to join Smith in Kentucky. The next ten days were a race for Kentucky between Bragg and Buell. Bragg won, getting north of his opponent. By September 18, he had his army set up facing south at Munfordville, Kentucky. The Confederate army was now 45 miles north of the Bowling Green defensive line that had been lost earlier in the year. They were also set up astride Buell's railroad line from Louisville in a strong defensive position along the Green River.

This was really the crucial point in the entire campaign. The Confederates had the initiative and if Smith had joined Bragg at Munfordville, Buell would have had a hard time dealing with the combined force. Smith and Bragg could also have joined together to make an attempt to seize Louisville, where the defenses were getting stronger each day. Instead, Bragg decided to pull back towards Smith's position. Bragg's army was low on food and forage and he could not remain long in Munfordville. If Buell did not attack him in short order, he feared that his army might starve. On September 20, Bragg directed his men to move northeast (towards Smith) to Bardstown.

When Buell received word of the Confederate withdrawal, he moved slowly from his position just south of Munfordville, and on September 24 his lead divisions reached Louisville.[3] On September 28, Bragg left his army under the charge of Major General Leonidas Polk while he traveled to Lexington to meet with Smith. For the time being, Bragg felt that he could live with Smith maintaining his separate position at Lexington; the Confederates could join together if, and when, Buell advanced from Louisville. Bragg and Smith would have been shocked to learn that the normally cautious Buell was already undertaking such a move.

Buell was under immense pressure from Washington to throw Bragg and Smith out of Kentucky. Lincoln had been dissatisfied with Buell's inability to prevent the invasion, and on September 29, Buell received an order for him to relinquish command to Major General George H. Thomas. Thomas wanted no part of it. Assuming command in the middle of a campaign was not to his liking. During this episode Buell seems to have finally gotten the message that he needed to fight the Confederates to keep his job, so he marched his men out of Louisville toward Bragg on October 1.

Buell's army marched in three columns along three different routes toward Bardstown. On the left was the I Corps under Major General Alexander McCook; in the center was the II Corps, under Major General Thomas L. Crittenden; and on the left was the III Corps, commanded by Major General Charles C. Gilbert. The column under Crittenden was also being supervised by Thomas. Buell also sent two divisions under Brigadier General Joshua W. Sill toward Frankfort. While the main intent of this last force was to protect the flank of the main attack, Sill's movement confused Bragg and Smith as to Buell's intentions. Over the next week, Bragg would be indecisive in his deployments as he tried to figure out where most of Buell's men were headed.

On October 2, convinced that Sill's men were the vanguard of Buell's main force, Bragg sent Polk orders to move north and hit Buell in the flank while Smith stopped him at Frankfort. Polk, however, had received enough scouting reports to believe that Buell's main advance was, instead, heading right for him. He disobeyed Bragg's order (which would have put Buell on his flank) and had his men retreat east toward Harrodsburg, by way of Perryville.

On October 4, Bragg left Frankfort (where he and Smith had been involved in a ceremony installing the Confederate governor of Kentucky) and traveled to Harrodsburg. By the time Smith met him there for a conference on the sixth, Bragg had finally realized that Buell was not headed for Frankfort. He now believed, incorrectly, that Buell was aiming at Harrodsburg. On October 7, he issued orders for all the Confederate forces to gather at Versailles, just east of the Kentucky River and about 20 miles north of Harrodsburg. Two of Polk's four divisions were at Harrodsburg, while the other two (commanded by Major General William J. Hardee) were lagging behind and still at Perryville.

Bragg believed that the column trailing Hardee into Perryville was merely a small part of Buell's entire force. He ordered Polk to take one of his two divisions back from Harrodsburg to Perryville and help Hardee get rid of this nuisance and then make their way to Versailles. Polk's other division at Harrodsburg would move to Versailles immediately.

So on October 7, the Union and Confederate commanders were in a strange and almost comical situation. Bragg believed that a small Union force was moving on Perryville and dealt with the threat accordingly. Buell who believed that all the Confederates, even Smith's, were at Perryville approached cautiously.

The Battle and the Acoustics

When Hardee received word of Bragg's plan, he wrote Bragg a note expressing his displeasure. Like a teacher lecturing a student, Hardee (the author of a widely used tactics manual) reminded Bragg that the basic rule of war was to "throw the masses of your troops on the fractions of the enemy." He advised him to either pull all his men to Versailles at once and wait for Buell or bring all his men to Perryville and attack him. By the time Bragg received Hardee's note, it was too late. A major battle was erupting at Perryville.

Two of Buell's three columns (the left under McCook and the right under Crittenden), which were delayed by bad roads and lack of water, stopped on the night of October 7 eight and ten miles from Perryville, respectively. Only the center column, under Gilbert, managed to reach the western outskirts of the town by nightfall.

One of the key features of the campaign was the continuing drought, which now made any source of water look inviting. The drought, months long now, had brought streams and rivers in the region to the point where they were "either totally dry or shrunken into little, heated, tired-looking threads of water, brackish and disagreeable to taste and smell."[4] About two miles to the west of Perryville was what was left of Doctor's Creek, a tributary of the Chaplin River. As Gilbert's tired and thirsty men approached Perryville, they found the creek guarded by snipers on a high ridge on the eastern bank. Twice on the evening of October 7 they attacked, trying to get to the water, and twice they were repelled. They bedded down that night astride the Springfield Road, knowing that precious water was only yards away.

On the morning of October 8, Polk arrived with one division and assumed command from Hardee. The Confederates now had about 16,000 men at Perryville. Neither Polk nor Hardee had a good idea of how many Union troops were across the ridges from their men. While trying to decide whether to attack, as Bragg desired, the Federals opened the battle by once again sending men forward to secure the water of Doctor's Creek. Brigadier General Philip H. Sheridan, in charge of one of Gilbert's divisions, succeeded not only in taking possession of the creek, but also of the ridge beyond Doctor's Creek to the east.

While glad to finally have access to water, Sheridan's push to the east alarmed Gilbert. He had been given orders from Buell not to bring on a general engagement until McCook's column came up the Mackville Road on his left and Crittenden's column came up on his right. After a reconnaissance to feel out the Confederate position, Buell hoped to attack with all three of his corps.[5] He sent orders to McCook and Thomas informing them that their troops should be in motion early enough to begin battle at Perryville by 7:00 A.M.

After Sheridan had held his ground for a while and more Confederate attacks did not seem to be coming, Gilbert was apparently satisfied that he had not accidentally started a major battle. He moved his other two divisions forward to join Sheridan on the ridge. He then rode back to Buell's headquarters, which had been set up on the Springfield Road about three miles west of Gilbert's position. Buell had been thrown by a horse and was convalescing at a house along the Springfield Road.

The other two columns made much slower progress than Buell had hoped, but eventually made their way to the outskirts of Perryville. At about 12:30 P.M., McCook arrived at Buell's headquarters (where Gilbert was already waiting) to inform him that his corps had arrived and was getting into position on the left. He also told Buell that he had seen no sign of the Confederates except for a few cavalry troopers. A quarter-mile-wide valley in a bend of Doctor's Creek separated his troops, coming down the Mackville Road, from Gilbert's men. By 1:00 P.M., Crittenden's column was also arriving, though Buell apparently did not yet know it. Buell now had an estimated 55,000 men west of Perryville.

On the Confederate side, Bragg had arrived from Harrodsburg at about 10:00 A.M., expecting to find Polk and Hardee pushing aside a small Union force. Polk informed him that the Union force across the way was probably much larger than they had previously thought and had actually attacked them earlier in the morning. In spite of the uncertainty in the size of their enemy, Polk suggested that they attempt to swing down on the Federal left flank. Bragg agreed, and by 1:00 P.M. the Confederate troops had been maneuvered into position for the attack.

The attack began in early afternoon with Confederate divisions under Brigadier General Simon Bolivar Buckner (hero of Fort Donelson) and Major General Benjamin Cheatham crashing in on McCook's Corps on the Union left. Simultaneously, an attack was made on Gilbert's Corps in the center by two brigades under Brigadier General James Patton Anderson. While Gilbert was able to fend off Anderson (whose attack was really a diversion, anyway), Buckner and Cheatham had great success against McCook. The Union troops, many in battle for the first time, were driven back more than a mile, losing 15 guns. McCook arrived on the scene, having ridden back from Buell's headquarters, completely amazed at what he was seeing. Not even knowing his corps was engaged, it was now collapsing right in front of him.

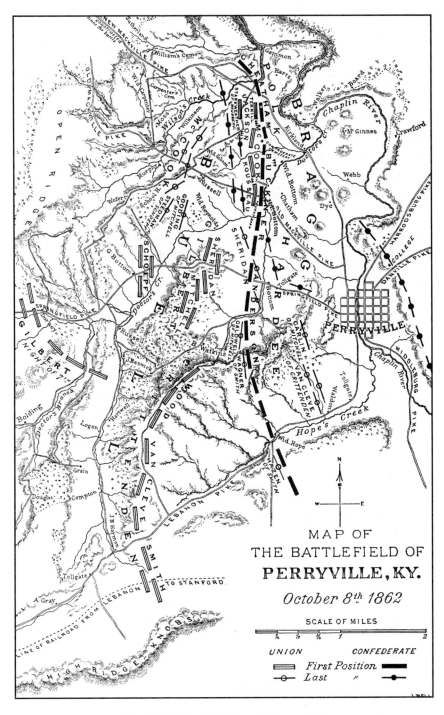

Fig. 7.5. The Battle of Perryville

Battles and Leaders of the Civil War

He frantically called for help from Gilbert, who sent two brigades, but no more. Gilbert and Sheridan were unsure of how many Confederates might come up against their line. As it turned out, their 20,000 men were being stalemated by only about twenty-five hundred under Anderson. Some of Sheridan's gunners did cause mayhem in the Confederate advance by firing shells into the flank of the attack. During all this time, Crittenden's entire column was for the most part unengaged. He had been bluffed by twelve hundred Confederate cavalry posted south of town.

The brutal fight on the Union left continued for more than two hours before Buell was aware that anything was happening. Back at his headquarters three miles from the battlefield, he had been bathed in silence, waiting for word from his commanders that their reconnaissance of the Confederate position had been completed. Around noon, he had actually decided to call off the attack for that day because of the delays in getting his men into position.[6] Throughout the rest of the afternoon, he and Gilbert heard occasional cannon shots, but nothing to indicate that a major battle was occurring three miles away.

Finally, around 4:00 P.M., Buell detected an increase in the intensity of the artillery fire. At around that same time, Captain Horace Fisher of McCook's Corps came riding up to inform Buell that McCook's men had been fighting for hours and were in danger of being enveloped.[7]

The sounds of the battle, as detected at Buell's headquarters, are best described by firsthand accounts. Buell describes the scene in *Battles and Leaders of the Civil War*:

> At 4 o'clock Captain Fisher of McCook's staff arrived and reported to me that the left corps had been sustaining a severe conflict for a considerable time, and was being driven back. I was astonished. Not a sound of musketry had been heard, and my staff-officers had been at the front until dinner-time. I had noticed a sudden increase of cannonading at 2 o'clock, and General Gilbert, who had come in from his lines and was getting his dinner with me, immediately proceeded to his command; but as the firing as suddenly subsided, and no report came to me, I had ceased to think of the occurrence.[8]

In his first report to Halleck, Buell wrote: "At 4 o'clock I received a request from General McCook for re-enforcements, and heard with astonishment that the left had been seriously engaged for several hours and that the right and left of that corps were being turned and severely pressed."[9]

In a formal report written later, Buell describes the scene in more detail: "The cannonading…became brisker as the day advanced, but was not supposed to proceed from any serious engagement, as no report to that effect was received."

> At 4 o'clock, however, Major General McCook's aide-de-camp arrived and reported to me that the general was sustaining a severe attack, which he would not be able to withstand unless re-enforced; that his flanks were already giving way. He added, to my astonishment, that the left corps had actually been engaged in a severe battle for several hours, perhaps since 12 o'clock. It was so difficult to credit the latter that I thought there must be some apprehension in regard to the former.[10]

Finally, in another account, Buell states that "…no sound of musketry reached my headquarters by which the sharpness of the action on the left could be known or even suspected, and when the fact was ascertained it was too late to do more than throw in succor before night set in."[11]

Though Buell recalled that Gilbert had left his headquarters before McCook's report arrived, Gilbert, also writing in *Battles and Leaders*, recalled that he was still present: "Owing to the conformation of the ground and to the limited use of artillery on both sides, no sound of the battle had been heard at General Buell's headquarters until the attack reached General Sheridan's position, which was about half-past 3 o'clock. Then the cannon firing became so continuous and was so well sustained and so different from the irregular shots, at wide intervals, which had characterized the 'shelling of the woods' earlier in the day, that it was readily recognized as a battle. It was near 4 o'clock when there came up the valley of Doctor's Creek the sound of rapid artillery firing. It was too heavy and too well sustained to come from merely 'shelling the woods.' Listening attentively for a moment, General Buell said to me, 'That is something more than shelling the woods; it sounds like a fight.' I at once mounted and set off at a rapid pace down the road in the direction of the firing."[12]

Whether Gilbert was present at Buell's headquarters at 4:00 P.M. or not, it is apparent that the sounds of the large battle three miles to the east did not reach Buell clearly. In addition, as described often in this book, a general who is not expecting a battle may not hear a battle, even when it is very close-by.

The propagation of sound around the attack on the Union left must have been unusual, even compared to that around other battles described in this book. As author Shelby Foote described it: " ...the six-mile-long scene of action (or nonaction) was compartmented, each sector being sealed off from the others as if by soundproof walls." This description is confirmed by the amazing account by Major J. Montgomery Wright, of Buell's staff. He was ordered by James Fry, Buell's chief of staff, to tell Gilbert to reinforce McCook:

> I did not know what was going on at the left, and Colonel Fry did not inform me. He told me what to say to General Gilbert, and to go fast, and taking one of the general's orderlies with me, I started on my errand. I found General Gilbert at the front, and as he had no staff-officer at hand at the moment, he asked me to go to General Schoepf, one of his division commanders, with the order. Schoepf promptly detached two brigades, and he told me I had better go on ahead and find out where they were to go. There was no sound to direct me, and as I tried to take an air line I passed outside the Union lines and was overtaken by a cavalry officer, who gave me the pleasing information that I was riding toward the enemy's pickets. Now up to this time I had heard no sound of battle; I had heard no artillery in front of me, and no heavy infantry-firing. I rode back, and passed behind the cavalry regiment which was deployed in the woods, and started in the direction indicated to me by the officer who called me back. At some distance I overtook an ambulance train, urged to its best speed, and then I knew that something serious was on hand. This was the first intimation I had that one of the fiercest struggles of the war was at that moment raging almost within my sight.

Directed by officers in charge of the ambulances I made another detour, and pushing on at greater speed I suddenly turned
into a road, and there before me, within a few hundred yards, the
battle of Perryville burst into view, and the roar of the artillery and
the continuous rattle of the musketry first broke upon my ear. It
was the finest spectacle I ever saw. It was wholly unexpected, and
it fixed me with astonishment. It was like tearing away a curtain
from the front of a great picture, or the sudden bursting of a thun-
der-cloud when the sky in front seems serene and clear. I had seen
an unlooked-for storm at sea, with hardly a moment's notice, hurl
itself out of the clouds and lash the ocean into a foam of wild rage.
But here there was not the warning of an instant. At one bound my
horse carried me from stillness into the uproar of battle. One turn
from a lonely bridlepath through the woods brought me face to
face with the bloody struggle of thousands of men.[13]

With such an account from a person right next to the battle, is
there little wonder that Buell could not hear the conflict? What could
cause such an amazing acoustic event? There is no mention of significant wind associated with the battle at Perryville. And in spite of the
limited use of artillery during the initial assault by Buckner and
Cheatham (when the cannons had trouble keeping up with waves of
Confederate infantry sweeping over McCook's position), most accounts
indicate that the battle, when it was heard, was quite loud. One veteran
of Shiloh said: "Such fighting I have never witnessed and in fact never
has been witnessed on the battlefields of America."[14] Bragg said that
"for the time engaged, it was the severest and most desperately con-
tested engagement within my knowledge."[15]

The most likely cause for the strange sounds of Perryville was
temperature-induced refraction, combined with effects of the terrain.
The weather on the day of the battle was hot and sunny, as it had been
for weeks. The ground was parched and there was certainly a hot layer
of air near the ground which would have refracted sounds strongly upward. The sharply undulating terrain of the battlefield, with ridges and
valleys running in all directions, would buffer sound waves that might
otherwise directly reach the listener or propagate along the ground.

Wright's account above indicates that McCook's battle was inaudible at places near Gilbert's position. Thomas, on the far Union right, reported hearing occasional rumbling of artillery.[16] In his report, Buell stated that the Union right flank (Crittenden's corps) was unaware of the severity of the attack on the left, six miles away.[17]

Earlier in the day, McCook reported hearing the sounds of Sheridan's battle not long after he began marching toward Perryville from Mackville.[18] At the point when he heard Sheridan's artillery, he was still more than five miles from Perryville. McCook's chief of staff, Captain Percival Oldershaw, also confirms this: "We had not proceeded far before we heard the booming of cannon in the distance."

It may have been that the battle was heard more easily at a distance, once one was away from the sharp ridges around Doctor's Creek. It may also have been that the sun had not yet built up a layer of hot air above the ground at that hour, so upward refraction was minimal.

By the time Buell was aware that he had been struck on the left, the battle was beginning to wind down. The Confederate wave was becoming disorganized and Sheridan's gunners, pouring in shells from the south, helped slow them down. McCook was eventually able to regain control of his shattered corps and began a back-and-forth struggle on the Union left that continued until darkness caused both sides to fall back.

The Aftermath

Buell had fought his first major battle and it had been a bust. Acoustics had kept him from even knowing that a battle was occurring; as a result only one of his three corps was really involved in the thick of the fighting. He had Bragg outnumbered almost three to one, and Bragg had come close to routing him. If Buell had been able to hear the attack on his left much earlier, he may have done Bragg serious damage.

During the night, Buell decided that at first light he would attempt his original plan of a simultaneous three-corps attack. Bragg, however, finally realized the odds he was facing. When Union troops moved cautiously forward on October 9, they found that Bragg and his men were gone.

Bragg had pulled back to Harrodsburg and ordered Kirby Smith and his men finally to join him there. Buell followed and on October 11, the two armies faced off at Harrodsburg. Now that he at last had all his men together, Bragg gave up on the entire campaign. He had expected men from Kentucky to enlist in his army by the tens of thousands, but had recruited only a trickle. He had carried 20,000 muskets with him for potential recruits, guns that never saw action. He knew that his men, having trouble surviving in the fall, would suffer terribly trying to live off the land in the winter. Bragg ordered a retreat to the southeast.

Day by day the gray column moved back toward Cumberland Gap, with Buell in close, but cautious pursuit. Buell found it hard to believe that Bragg was actually leaving the state and not just maneuvering for better position from which to make another attack. But by October 22, the Confederates had passed through Cumberland Gap. Buell did not pursue farther. Lincoln and Halleck, dismayed that Buell did not maintain the pursuit to clear eastern Tennessee of Confederates, sent a telegraph on October 24 ordering Buell to turn his command over to Rosecrans.

Bragg and Rosecrans would clash twice in the upcoming year. Bragg would move his force back toward Nashville later in 1862, and would fight a bloody battle with Rosecrans at Murfreesboro on New Year's Day. Rosecrans got the best of him that day; however, Bragg would get his revenge in September 1863, beating Rosecrans at Chickamauga.

Though Bragg's invasion was not the smashing success for which he hoped, it had served the purpose of setting back the Union's invasion of the South by some months. And the strange sounds of Perryville had almost given him one of the South's greatest victories.

Chapter 8

Chancellorsville, Virginia

In what may have been the high point in Confederate military history, Robert E. Lee and Stonewall Jackson combined in a flank attack that stunned the Army of the Potomac and its commander, Joe Hooker. An acoustic shadow caused by the dense foliage of the Wilderness added to Hooker's confusion.

Background

As the year 1863 began, the overall situation for the Confederacy was not good. The Mississippi River was almost totally controlled by the Union, leaving only a few points of connection between the Trans-Mississippi and the rest of the Confederacy. General Braxton Bragg had retreated from Kentucky and was now losing at Murfreesboro, giving up most of Tennessee. The Union naval blockade continued to tighten.

In Virginia, however, the Army of Northern Virginia under General Robert E. Lee had managed to hold its own and then some. After a brutal draw at Antietam in September 1862, the Confederates had sullenly withdrawn back to Virginia. The delay in the Federal pursuit persuaded Abraham Lincoln to sack McClellan for good, and Major General Ambrose E. Burnside replaced him, somewhat reluctantly.

Burnside was not anxious to take command of the Army of the Potomac because, as he had told Lincoln on two other occasions when the job had been offered, he felt he was not competent to take charge of such a large force. He agreed this time because the alternative choice was Major General Joseph Hooker, one of the few men that Burnside disliked. Burnside's feelings for Hooker were apparently widespread in the Army of the Potomac, with many fellow officers feeling that Hooker, though a hard fighter, was too ambitious and egotistical.

After taking over for the popular McClellan in early November, 1862, Burnside moved into action. Lee's army was separated into two corps, separated by 40 miles and the Blue Ridge Mountains. The Union army was closer to either of these corps than they were to each other. In what was probably a blunder, and in opposition to Lincoln's wishes, Burnside decided to make the Confederate capital of Richmond his objective instead of aiming for Lee's battered soldiers. He planned to sidestep Lee by moving east to Fredericksburg, crossing the Rappahannock River there and then marching south. There are also some indications that Burnside may have actually wanted to winter near Fredericksburg and then repeat McClellan's movement up the eastern Virginia Peninsula.[1]

Burnside began to move his men on November 15, and when Major General Edwin Sumner's Corps arrived, they found the town lightly guarded. Though lacking pontoons, Sumner asked Burnside if he could cross at a nearby ford, but the request was denied. Burnside was apparently afraid that Lee would pounce on any part of his army that might be caught alone on the south side of the river. By November 20, the window of easy opportunity was closed, as one of Lee's Corps (under Lieutenant General James Longstreet) had arrived to defend the town.

Burnside's army continued to fill the heights at Falmouth opposite Fredericksburg, but by the time his pontoons finally arrived on November 25, the Union general could see that the Confederates had thrown up earthworks behind the town. As he delayed still longer to conduct a more detailed reconnaissance, Lee's other corps (under Lieutenant General Thomas "Stonewall" Jackson) arrived on November 29.

Jackson's men were posted southeast of the city. When Union balloon observations detected Jackson's presence, Burnside decided on a battle strategy.[2] He would attack at Fredericksburg to drive a wedge between the two wings of the Confederate army. On December 10, orders were issued for a crossing that night. Stubborn resistance by Southern sharpshooters delayed the Union bridge construction, enough so that by the time most of the Union forces crossed over on December 12, Lee had been able to consolidate his deployments.

Though Lee's position was vulnerable to being turned on either flank, Burnside insisted on attacking the center, where the position was so strong as to be almost impregnable. Earthworks, a sunken road, and a prominent hill for artillery provided an almost perfect defense against a frontal assault. Again and again on December 13, waves of brave Union soldiers hurled themselves against the Confederate line, only to be thrown back with heavy losses. By the time the day ended, the Army of the Potomac had endured its most crushing defeat.

After several of his generals traveled to Washington in late December to complain to Lincoln that Burnside had lost the army's confidence, Burnside tendered his resignation. Lincoln, however, refused the resignation and set Burnside back to work. In late January, Burnside decided to try another means of getting at Lee. He would travel upriver and cross the Rappahannock, coming down on Lee's left flank.

It was a better plan; unfortunately, the weather refused to cooperate: a cold rain set in as soon as the movement upriver had commenced. Men, mules, and wagons sunk into the rivers of mud that had once been roads. By the time Burnside gave up and called his men back, the Mud March had become the low point in the history of the Army of the Potomac. Confederates across the river laughed, yelled, and held up humorous signs as the Union men trudged back to their camps.

The frustrated Burnside turned his wrath on the generals that he felt had betrayed him to Lincoln and had continued to poison his attempts to run the army. In particular, he singled out Hooker, who had made it widely known to reporters that he felt Burnside's plans were absurd.[3] He gave Lincoln an ultimatum: either dismiss Hooker and several other generals or Burnside would resign. On January 25, Lincoln announced his decision. He would accept Burnside's resignation and Hooker would now command the Army of the Potomac.

Even Hooker's enemies had to admit that he did an excellent job in the first three months of command. In Hooker's own words, the force over which he took control was "an unhappy army, defeated, despondent, ravaged by desertion, unpaid, and stuck in the mud..."[4] As Hooker said, the desertion rate was high. He attacked the problem by instituting a scheme of rotating furloughs, earned through soldierly conduct. He also had a few deserters shot as examples, and prohibited future

Fig. 8.1. Joseph Hooker

Library of Congress

shipments of civilian clothing to the soldiers from their relatives. Many had been using these clothes to successfully sneak away from the army.

Hooker overhauled a corrupt commissary system that had been siphoning food for profit and leaving many soldiers hungry in the midst of plenty. He also created a system of insignias for each of the corps of the army, with the aim of boosting morale and also of identifying and embarrassing stragglers in the field. Slowly, the life came back into the Army of the Potomac. As one soldier wrote: "...never was the magic influence of a single man more clearly shown."[5]

Hooker also made two important changes in military operations. First, he began the operation of a sophisticated system of agents operating behind Confederate lines. Prior to this, the Union army had been mostly in the dark about Lee's deployments and numbers. Hooker also organized the Union cavalry into three divisions. Before, the horsemen had been dispersed throughout the various corps and divisions, and rarely had the chance to operate in a cohesive and effective manner. On St. Patrick's Day, the Union cavalrymen met their Confederate counterparts at Kelly's Ford, 20 miles up the Rappahannock. Though the resulting drawn battle is best remembered for the death of Confederate artilleryman John Pelham, it was also a turning point for Union cavalry. On that day they finally matched the Southern cavalry, and their spirits soared as they looked forward to the spring campaign.

In early April, Lincoln came to the Union camps for a visit, and Hooker staged a grand review. Four of his seven corps paraded by Lincoln like a well-oiled machine, in step and bayonets gleaming. Lincoln was impressed with the soldiers and they were impressed with themselves. Hooker said: "If the enemy does not run, God help them."[6]

After Lincoln returned to Washington, he and Hooker exchanged their thoughts on the upcoming campaign. Hooker's plan was to send his confident cavalry on a long mission riding far to the west of Lee and then looping down around him to the south. Meanwhile, Hooker would send infantry up the Rappahannock to sweep down on Lee from the west while other infantry held Lee in place by crossing at Fredericksburg. Lee would either be destroyed at Fredericksburg or would flee south where he would run into the Union cavalry. In his own words:

> I have concluded that I will have more chance of inflicting a heavier blow upon the enemy by turning his position to my right, and if practicable, to sever his communications with Richmond with my dragoon force and such light batteries as it may be advisable to send with him. I am apprehensive that he will retire from before me the moment I succeed in crossing the river, and over the shortest line to Richmond, and thus escape being seriously crippled. I hope that when the cavalry have established themselves on the line between him and Richmond, they will be able to hold him and check his retreat until I can fall on his rear, or, if not, that I will compel him to fall back by the way of Culpeper and Gordonsville, over a longer line than my own, with his supplies cut off. The cavalry will probably cross the river above the Rappahannock Bridge, thence to Culpeper and Gordonsville and across the Aquia Railroad, somewhere in the vicinity of Hanover Court-House. They will probably have a fight in the vicinity of Culpeper, but not one that should cause them much delay or embarrassment. I have given directions for the cavalry to be in readiness to commence the movement on Monday morning next. While the cavalry are moving I shall threaten the passage of the river at various points, and after they have passed well to the enemy's rear, shall endeavor to effect the crossing.[7]

After dealing with Burnside, Hooker's confidence must have been something of a relief to Lincoln. Still, he had heard it all before from George McClellan and John Pope, neither of whom had fulfilled their boasts. Lincoln approved the plan and sat back to await the outcome.

It was a good plan, and would have to be to defeat the crafty Lee. Aiding the plan would be the weakened numbers in Lee's army. In mid-February, he had sent a quarter of his men (half of Longstreet's Corps) down to southeastern Virginia. There had been threats of a Union corps moving in that direction, and the move would also serve to ease the food and forage problems facing the Confederates at Fredericksburg. Hooker's new intelligence network promptly informed him of the movement.

Lee was still perplexed as to Hooker's intentions. Would he try to take Fredericksburg or move to the rail junction at Gordonsville? In any event, he informed Jefferson Davis that if Hooker did not move by May 1, the Confederates would have to do so. Both men and horses were low on food, and moving the campaign to the Shenandoah Valley would ease things considerably. Longstreet's men could be brought back to defend Fredericksburg.

Hooker made these considerations a moot point by going into action in late April. He put his troops into action in a more effective way than any commander of the Army of the Potomac had before. On April 27, the Union XI Corps (under Major General Oliver O. Howard), XII Corps (under Major General Henry Slocum), and V Corps (under Major General George Meade) began to move up the Rappahannock's north bank. Unlike Burnside's ponderous movement, the Union men moved quickly and far back from the river, out of sight of the Confederate pickets. Strict silence was maintained.

At Kelly's Ford, Hooker had had pontoon boats hidden. On the night of April 28, Union engineers laid the boats out and covered them with pine boughs to muffle the sounds of the crossing men and artillery. By dawn the next day, the

Fig. 8.2. Robert E. Lee
Library of Congress

XI and XII Corps had crossed the Rappahannock. Major General J.E.B. Stuart's Confederate cavalry had been kept at a distance by Union pickets so that Lee had little information regarding the movement. When Stuart captured a foreign observer riding with the XI Corps, he telegraphed Lee that Federal troops were across the river. Stuart guessed, though, that they were probably headed to Gordonsville.

By the evening of April 29, all three Union corps involved in the flanking movement had crossed both the Rappahannock and Rapidan Rivers (Howard and Slocum crossed the Rapidan at Germanna Ford and Meade crossed farther east at Ely's Ford). Farther to the east, the Union I and VI Corps were crossing the Rappahannock south of Fredericksburg.

Hooker's plan was working perfectly. The only sizable Confederate infantry west of Chancellorsville were the brigades of Brigadier Generals William Mahone and Carnot Posey, guarding the United States Ford, about eight miles west of Fredericksburg. On the afternoon of April 29, two riders rushed into the Confederate camps at U.S. Ford to inform the generals that a large Union force was rolling in from the west. Posey and Mahone realized that this made their position guarding the ford untenable, and withdrew to a position guarding the Ely's Ford Road and the Orange Turnpike, just west of Chancellorsville.

Chancellorsville was not a town, but the site of a large mansion that served as both the home of the Chancellor family and as a popular roadhouse for travelers. It was situated at the intersection of the Ely's Ford Road and the Orange Turnpike and just to the east of the point (at Wilderness Church) where the Orange Plank Road joined the turnpike. The location was about eight miles west of Fredericksburg, and three miles south of U.S. Ford.

Hooker had expected that his flanking movement would uncover U.S. Ford. As the Confederates pulled back, he had the II Corps, under Major General Darius Couch, ready to cross there. He now had four Union corps moving on Lee's left flank, with Lee mostly unaware of what was happening. Howard, Slocum, Meade, and Couch drove their men as hard as they could.

The progress of the Union flanking movement was slowed to a great extent, however, by the nature of the terrain. The only way to push east to Chancellorsville was along the roads running from the Rapidan and Rappahannock fords. The ground surrounding the roads was covered with an extremely dense second-growth forest called The Wilderness by the locals. Iron furnaces were spotted throughout the region and as they consumed wood, new trees and shrubs grew. This had been going on for over one hundred fifty years, and the resulting mess of stumps, oaks, pines, and briars was almost impenetrable.[8] It was much like the terrain near Fort Donelson, Iuka, and Seven Pines, and probably worse. Without cavalry protection on the flanks, thousands of men moved in narrow columns on the roads converging at Chancellorsville.

By the night of April 29, Stuart had finally seen enough to convince him that a major flanking movement was occurring, so he relayed the news to Lee. Lee, in turn, wired Jefferson Davis: "Their intention, I presume, is to turn our left, and probably to get into our rear. Our scattered condition favors their operations. I hope if any reinforcements can be sent, they may be forwarded immediately." The scattered condition to which Lee referred was the absence of Longstreet and half his command. Over the next few days, Lee would plead for Longstreet to be sent to him, but without success.

Lee immediately ordered Major General Richard H. Anderson to take a brigade west from Fredericksburg to join Mahone and Posey near Chancellorsville. When Anderson arrived, he decided to pull back the Confederate position a few miles east of Chancellorsville to allow open fields for shooting at the Yankees. In the early morning of April 30, Anderson, Posey, and Mahone skirmished with Union cavalry as they dropped back to a new line near Tabernacle Church.

By afternoon on April 30, Hooker had nearly 50,000 men at or near the Chancellorsville crossroads. Meade, who was first to arrive, hailed Slocum as the XII Corps arrived:

> This is splendid, Slocum! Hurrah for old Joe! We're on Lee's flank, and he doesn't know it. You take the Plank Road toward Fredericksburg, and I'll take the Pike, or vice versa, as you prefer, and we will get out of this Wilderness.

In Hooker's original orders, Slocum was to drive on toward Banks' Ford, which was only about four miles from Fredericksburg. Only one Confederate brigade, under Brigadier General Cadmus M. Wilcox, guarded the ford. By taking the ford, Hooker would then use it as a crossing point. The two wings of his army (the flanking wing and the wing crossing at Fredericksburg) would then be within easy reach of each other. Lee would be in serious trouble.

It was here that Hooker made his first mistake of the campaign. He decided to halt his men near Chancellorsville to regroup. He had the jump on Lee and had more than twice as many men. It didn't seem possible to Hooker that a brief rest could alter the outcome much. He was wrong.

As Hooker arrived on the scene, his generals, following his orders, had formed the Union forces into a defensive arc. Couch and the II Corps stretched from the Rappahannock to near Chancellorsville. Meade's men faced east in a clearing near the Chancellor mansion, with Slocum's men then placed in an arc that faced first east and then south. The Union position finished with Howard's men facing south in a line along the Orange Turnpike.

Despite the halt to the flanking movement, most of the soldiers were in fine spirits. For once, they had gotten the best of Lee. Hooker was ecstatic: "The rebel army…is now the legitimate property of the Army of the Potomac. They may as well pack up their haversacks and make for Richmond. I shall be after them…"[9]

Lee gave Anderson orders to dig in; he would send reinforcements if possible. He also told Anderson to have his men ready to move out at a moment's notice in case he called for a general retreat. By the afternoon of April 30, though, Lee had decided on his response to Hooker's operation. Although outnumbered, he would defy military doctrine and split his own force. He would leave one brigade in Fredericksburg (under Brigadier General William Barksdale), positioned about where the defenses had been during the December battle. Another brigade (under Brigadier General Jubal Early) would confront the Union corps crossing below the town. All the rest of the Confederates would head west to meet Hooker's flank attack.

The boldness of the move still amazes students of the battle. Near Fredericksburg, 10,000 Confederates would go up against more than 45,000 Union men. At Chancellorsville, Lee would be outnumbered by about 80,000 to 40,000. Most commanders would retreat rather than fight their way out of such a trap. But Lee had supreme confidence in his men and in his subordinate commanders, especially Stonewall Jackson. He ordered Jackson to take charge of the Confederate defenses at Tabernacle Church. Before dawn on May 1, Jackson's men were moving out.

Thaddeus Lowe, observing from a Union balloon north of the Rappahannock, noted the movement of Jackson's column. He also noted that there appeared to be as many men as usual still in the vicinity of Fredericksburg. A rebel deserter (possibly planted by Lee) informed Union officers that Longstreet was on his way to join Lee.[10] This would be the beginning of days of confusion on the part of the Union command as to the location and numbers for the various parts of Lee's army.

Jackson arrived near Tabernacle Church at about 8:00 A.M. and took command from Anderson. Anderson had started his men digging earthworks during the night. Jackson, though realizing that he was greatly outnumbered, decided the best defense against the Union juggernaut would be an attack. He told Anderson to have his men stop digging and get ready to move out.

By 11:00 A.M., the Confederates were moving. One column, commanded by Major General Lafayette McLaws, headed straight toward Chancellorsville along the Orange Turnpike. Jackson would lead a larger column along the Orange Plank Road, which dipped south for a bit and then met the turnpike again at Chancellorsville.

The Union army was also moving. Hooker had decided to break free of the Wilderness and smash through any small Confederate force between him and Fredericksburg. Meade and his V Corps would move along the River Road to Banks's Ford, while the XII and XI Corps would move straight down the turnpike.

Within 15 minutes, the skirmishers on each side were picking each other off along the turnpike as the blue and gray columns collided. Slowly, the Union troops fell back from each of the Confederate columns, but in good order. Along the River Road, Meade cruised along without much opposition toward Banks's Ford.

The Union retreat along the turnpike and Plank Road finally stopped in a fairly good position, with a clear field of fire in front. It was then that the generals on the field got an order from Hooker (still back at the Chancellor mansion) to pull back toward the Chancellor clearing and assume the positions of the previous night. Hooker was shocked that Lee (actually Jackson) was aggressively confronting him this far west of Fredericksburg.

Meade was making good progress on the River Road and was within sight of Banks's Ford when he got the order to go back. He was furious, as were the generals closer to Chancellorsville. If Meade had continued on to the ford and taken it (almost a certainty given how lightly it was defended), the outcome of the battle would probably have been far different. But Hooker had been put on the spot and his reaction was to back down and assume a defensive posture.

Lee now rode west to assume command of the forces confronting Hooker. He directed Early to hold out against attack as long as possible and to not give away how few men were now manning the Confederate lines around Fredericksburg. If pushed out of his defenses, Early was to fall back to the south to protect the army's supply trains. If the Federal pressure around the town proved not to be great, Early was to send as many men as possible to fight near Chancellorsville.

By late afternoon on Friday, May 1, Hooker had apparently decided to wait in his defenses, hoping that Lee would attack. Using shovels, bayonets, cups and plates, the men added to the earthworks and fortifications that they had begun the previous night. The euphoria among the troops about fooling Lee must have dissipated as the men realized that they were now on the defensive.

When Lee arrived to Jackson's position, the two generals conferred about the best way to get at Hooker. True to form, neither man regarded retreat as an option. At first, Lee contemplated a direct assault on Hooker's main line at Chancellorsville. But late in the afternoon, the rebel cavalry brought in some most interesting news.

The Federal right flank, manned by the XI Corps, was "up in the air": not anchored on any natural feature. If the Confederates could get to that flank, they could attack the entire Union position from flank and rear. There would be great risk in the attempt, though. Lee had already split his outnumbered army. To do so again would invite disaster. If Hooker discovered that a considerable number of the Confederates at Chancellorsville were moving around the Union flank, he could attack and destroy Lee at almost any point.

Still, Lee believed it was worth the attempt. He sent Stuart with a local guide to find out if there was a way around to the Union flank that would be out of Hooker's sight. When Lee found out later in the night that there were back roads that would serve his purpose, he again met with Jackson. Jackson had driven his men on a classic flank march prior to the smashing Confederate victory at Second Manassas the previous summer. Could he do it again?

Lee and Jackson looked at a rough sketch of the various roads in the vicinity. Jackson pointed out the road he thought best for the flanking movement. Lee asked him with how many men he planned to make the attack. Jackson replied: "With my whole corps." With that statement, which may have surprised even the bold Lee, began one of history's greatest surprise attacks. Jackson would take about 28,000 men, leaving Lee with only about 14,000 to face Hooker's 65,000.[11] Jackson hoped to be marching by 4:00 A.M.

Jackson's men were not prepared to march, and it was almost 7:00 A.M. before his lead regiments began filing down the back roads south of Chancellorsville. The route led west from the Orange Plank Road until reaching the Catharine Furnace, at which point the road dipped south. It continued south and then southwest for about two miles before intersecting with the Brock Road. The Brock Road ran in a north-south line and intersected both the Orange Plank Road and the Orange Turnpike about two miles west of Hooker's right flank.

Fig. 8.3. Thomas "Stonewall" Jackson

When Jackson reached the Brock Road, he decided that in order to keep his troops from the eyes of the Yankee pickets he would follow a small road that paralleled the Brock Road. To reach this trail, which ran to the west of the Brock Road, he had his men turn south on the Brock Road

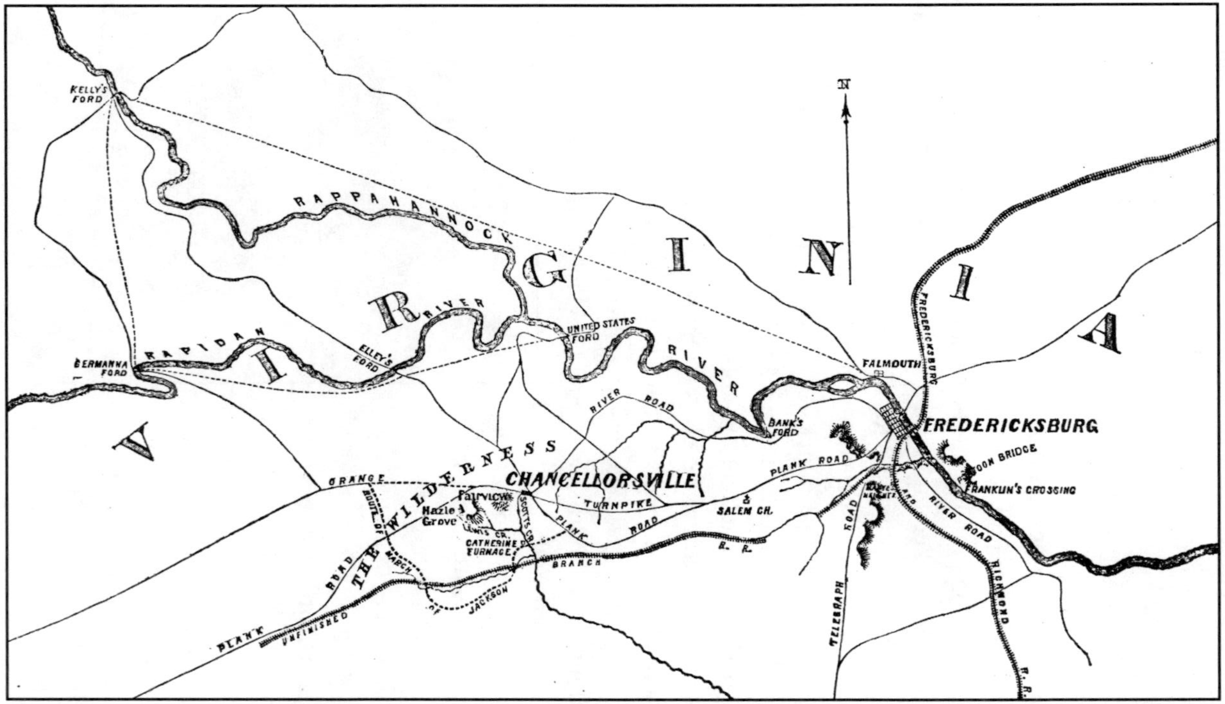

Fig. 8.4. The Chancellorsville Region

Draper, *History of the American Civil War*

for a little less than a mile and then march north on the side road. The side road then rejoined the Brock Road about a mile south of the Orange Plank Road. Jackson planned to launch his flank attack down the Orange Plank Road.

As his men filed down the road toward Catharine Furnace, their movement did not go unnoticed by the Union commanders. The entire column would stretch for more than five miles when all the troops were finally in motion. It almost defied logic that a commander would leave his force so vulnerable; if the long column was attacked at any point, there would be little room to deploy to make a defense. Union pickets located at a clearing called Hazel Grove noticed Jackson's troops early in the march. They could see the Confederate line heading toward Catharine Furnace, dipping out of sight into the valley of Scott Run, and then reappearing marching southward.

Hooker wondered at the meaning of this. His initial reaction, true to his old form, was that Lee was beating a retreat toward Gordonsville. Still, he had enough doubt that he sent a message to Howard at about 9:30 A.M. telling him to be prepared if the Confederates were moving on the Union flank.[12] It is not clear whether this message ever reached Howard.

The imbalance in numbers near the Chancellor mansion was growing greater. While most of Lee's men were now heading off with Jackson around Hooker's flank, Hooker had ordered Major General John Reynolds to bring his I Corps back across the river below Fredericksburg to join his force at Chancellorsville.

After Jackson's column had been observed passing Catharine Furnace for more than three hours, Union Major General Dan Sickles could stand it no longer. He asked permission from Hooker to drive one of his divisions into the Confederates. In the early afternoon of May 2, Sickles sent his men to try and pierce the gray column and a furious fight ensued around Catharine Furnace. With reinforcements sent from Lee (who was now left with next to nothing to face Hooker's force), Sickles's men were pushed back. Sickles reported to Hooker that he had done the column great damage but that most of it was now beyond his reach to the south.

This news elated Hooker: He had forced Bobby Lee into an ignominious retreat. He sent word to John Sedgwick at Fredericksburg to push into whatever forces were still at Fredericksburg. He also told Sedgwick: "We know that the enemy is fleeing, trying to save his trains. Two of Sickles' divisions are among them." It sounded as if the Army of Northern Virginia was in full rout. Union cavalry should be to the south by now, ready to play anvil to Hooker's hammer.

Meanwhile, Jackson was pressing his men on with his fierce determination. He did not allow even the usual 10-minute rest per hour of marching. Despite his efforts to conceal the march, a number of soldiers in Howard's Corps noted the Confederates moving on their flank. Their efforts to alert their commanders went unheeded. Hooker's belief that the enemy was in full retreat seemed to pervade the Union high command. Here was the point in the battle at which Hooker sorely missed his cavalry, sent on their long excursion toward Richmond. A large force was preparing to launch into his right flank, and he had no horsemen to monitor the movement. On the other side, Stuart's troopers did a credible job of screening the march from most Union eyes.

When Jackson arrived at the intersection of the Brock Road and the Orange Plank Road a little before 3:00 P.M., Brigadier General Fitzhugh Lee of Stuart's cavalry met him. Lee informed him (and showed him by leading Jackson to a good vantage point) that the Union flank extended a bit farther west than previously believed. Attacking down the Orange Plank Road would not put the Confederates fully on the Union flank. To get around the flank, the attack would have to come down the turnpike. This would mean another hour or two of marching. Jackson sent word to his men to keep heading up the Brock Road until reaching the turnpike.

It was a little after 5:00 P.M. before Jackson got his men organized for the attack. He arranged his men into three attacking waves, spread across a front of more than two miles. As they swept into the (mostly) unsuspecting XI Corps, his men would not only be on the Union flank but also in the rear of Hooker's position. It was a general's dream. At some point between 5:00 P.M. and 6:00 P.M., Jackson gave the order to move forward.

Jackson's men would have to move in unison through the Wilderness, the tangled forest thought to be impassable by the Union commanders. But these were mostly country boys and they made good progress. As the soldiers of Howard's XI settled down to enjoy their dinners, with arms stacked, they began to notice a rush of wildlife streaming out of the forest, flushed by the thousands of men tramping through it. A moment later a hellish fire of musketry blew through the Union camp. The attack had begun.

The Battle and the Acoustics

Many Union men were killed where they sat. Others managed to take off toward the east. A few managed to grab their rifles and attempt to make a stand. For years there was harsh criticism of the men and commanders of the XI Corps (many of German background) for their performance at Chancellorsville. But in retrospect it is likely that no men could have withstood the onslaught that came down on the XI Corps from flank and rear.

If Howard did indeed receive Hooker's message, the blame for the rout must rest mainly on him. Except for a small section of his line "refused" to the north, he had made little attempt to prepare for an attack on his flank. Like the rest of the Union generals, he must have been misled by the thought that Lee was in retreat and also by the presumed impossibility of any large force making its way through the Wilderness. In his defense, once the attack began he stood firm and made every possible attempt to rally his men. It was not enough.

The Confederates rolled through the XI Corps, killing, wounding, or capturing any man that remained in their path. Any pockets of resistance were quickly extinguished. Exacerbating the situation for the Union was the absence of Sickles's men and others along the turnpike line that had been sent to reinforce him. While these men remained near Catharine Furnace, the XI Corps found little support as they fled to the east. All the while, Stonewall Jackson rode with his men, driving them ever onward. The march to the Union flank had taken longer than expected and darkness was closing in.

At the Chancellor mansion, Hooker remained optimistic, probably pondering the glory that would result when he captured Lee and his army. He was about to be stunned. What happened next is described well by Confederate artillery officer Edward Porter Alexander:

> It was nearly 6 P.M. when the signal for the advance was given by a bugle, and taken up and repeated for each brigade by bugles

to the right and left through the woods. But the sounds seem to have been smothered in the forest, for the Federal reports make no mention of them. Their first intimation of anything unusual was given by wild turkeys, foxes, and deer, startled by the long lines of infantry and driven through the Federal camps.[13]

Alexander continues:

A notable case of acoustic shadows occurred during this action. Sickles, some two and a half miles away, heard nothing of the attack upon Howard until word was brought him, which he at first refused to believe. At 6:30 P.M., Hooker sat on the veranda of the Chancellorsville house in entire confidence that Lee was retreating to Gordonsville and that Sickles was 'among his trains.' Faint sounds of distant cannonading were at first supposed to come from Sickles. Presently, an aide looking down the road with his glass suddenly shouted, 'My God! Here they come.' All sprang to their horses and, riding down the road, met, in a half-mile, the fugitive rabble of Howard's corps, and learned that Jackson, with half of Lee's army, had routed the Federal flank.[14]

Modern author John Bigelow Jr. describes the same scene: "While Jackson was rolling up and crushing the Federal right, Hooker with his two aides, Candler and Russell, sat on the veranda of the Chancellor House, enjoying the summer evening. Now and then a shot came from the south and east, where Lee was keeping up a show of force, but nothing occurred to give them anxiety. Not a sound of the fighting at the Taylor Farm or even at the Wilderness Church had reached them. Not an officer from the forces attacked had come to them for aid, or to warn them of the impending danger, and so the hours passed until between 6:15 and 6:30..., when the sound of distant cannonading came to their ears, which they attributed to the movements of Birney's force. In Hancock's line it was thought that Stoneman's cavalry or some other Federal force had come up in the rear of a body of the enemy and was driving it toward the Federal lines. The shells, which came sailing through the air toward Chancellorsville from the northwest, were thought to be fired by pursuing Federals. Hooker and his staff were listening attentively and speculating as to the result of Sickles's operations, when Captain Russell stepped out in front, and turned his spyglass, with some trepidation, it would seem, in the direction of Dowdall's Tavern. A moment later he shouted to General Hooker: 'My God, here they come!' meaning Birney's men."[15]

Other accounts indicate that others near the Chancellor mansion were caught in the same acoustic shadow as Hooker and his staff. Author Stephen W. Sears states: "By some fluke of acoustics the roar of Jackson's assault did not immediately reach Federal headquarters at the Chancellor house. Or perhaps the banging of Lee's guns and those at Catharine Furnace drowned out the firing to the west."[16]

In an older book, Augustus Hamlin, historian of the XI Corps, also comments on the acoustics at Chancellorsville and elsewhere:

> It is also strange that the sounds of the distant conflict were not heard, or were too confused and indistinct to awaken suspicion. The noise of the battle did not seem to extend far. Sound has some remarkable characteristics, and in certain conditions of the atmosphere fails to refract or convey its waves to any considerable distance. The writer at one time noticed the batteries on Morris Island playing upon Sumter and Wagner, and heard no sounds of the explosions, although the guns were less than a third of a mile distant, yet the same artillery not long after awoke him at Beaufort, fifty miles away. The failure of the fog signals has also been observed and studied in connection with this peculiarity.
>
> McLaws, with his Confederate division, was waiting to hear the sounds of Jackson's guns before attacking Hancock with vigor. Posey and Wright, with their brigades concealed in the woods on Birney's flank, were listening for the same signal, but failed to hear definite sounds. Sickles, also, at the Welford Furnace, did not hear a sound of the fight which wrecked the Eleventh Corps, and was not aware of it until an hour or more after Jackson's men had driven the Federal troops back from the Dowdall Tavern.[17]

These comments make it clear that the acoustics around the Chancellorsville battlefield were poor. Neither Hooker nor Sickles at their respective locations were able to distinguish the sounds of Jackson's attack from other noises present at the time though each man was never more than a couple of miles from the fighting. The Confederates near Lee's headquarters also seem to have been unable to hear the attack until it got close to the Chancellorsville clearing.

A Union lieutenant sent into the woods near the point of Jackson's initial contact with the XI Corps just before the attack could not make out sounds clearly even from less than a mile away. He stated that he "began to hear a queer jumble of sounds, a confusion of orders." He could also occasionally hear notes of Confederate bugles, but not continuously.[18]

There is little doubt that the poor acoustics associated with the Battle of Chancellorsville must have been due to the thick foliage in the region. The weather at the time of the attack was pleasant, near 80 degrees.[19] There was a fairly strong wind blowing, but this would have had little effect in the dense Wilderness.

There was little artillery used by either side during the attack, as cannons would be confined to move either along the Orange Plank Road or the Orange Turnpike. Any noise they would have made was probably overwhelmed by the sounds booming from Lee's guns on the other side of Chancellorsville. He had been demonstrating against Hooker's line all afternoon to divert Union attention. Thus, the attack was mainly one involving small arms, whose sounds would have been heavily absorbed by the trees and leaves of the forest.

Strangely enough, sounds in the region appear to have carried better at longer distances than shorter. This was most likely due to sounds that escaped the treetops, only to be refracted down to earth farther away. For example, Union soldiers at Fredericksburg heard the St. Patrick's Day cavalry battle at Kelly's Ford.[20] Lee and Sedgwick, near Fredericksburg, both heard the opening guns near Chancellorsville on May 1.[21] Cadmus Wilcox, stationed at Banks's Ford, could hear the guns of Lee's diversionary attack on May 2.[22] There is at least one report that just before the flank attack on May 2, Jackson was able to hear Lee's guns to the east, though Lee would apparently be unable to hear Jackson's.[23]

May 2 was windy above the treeline, as witnessed by the grounding of Thaddeus Lowe's Union observation balloons during most of the day. (This, along with problems in the Union field telegraph system, contributed much to Hooker's confusion that day.)[24] The weather during the campaign had been mostly clear, with cool nights and foggy mornings, so a temperature inversion effect may have aided the wind in refracting sounds to earth over some distance.

The Aftermath

In the immediate aftermath of the acoustic shadow, Hooker acted promptly and courageously, helping to set up a line of defense west of Chancellorsville against the advancing Confederate wave. His position was still in great danger: Jackson and Lee were now situated less than two miles apart. If they could link together, Hooker would be under attack from three sides. But Hooker had nature on his side, as darkness began to throw Jackson's men into even greater disorder than that caused naturally by the Wilderness. Worse for Jackson, his men were exhausted. A full day's march in the heat, followed by a wild running fight through the woods, had taken its toll.

Jackson knew that during the night Hooker could regroup and regain his advantage, and continued to push his men, constantly seeking for a way to break the Union line and push the Yankees into the Rappahannock. As he and his staff returned from a reconnaissance between the lines, men from the 18th North Carolina accidentally shot him. He was carried from the field and died a week later. Jackson's forces were placed under Stuart, whom Lee trusted, but who had never before commanded infantry.

Hooker had his men begin building fortifications along a new, U-shaped line that ran along two streams and was backed by the river, with both of his bridges protected. He would fall back to this line if Stuart and Lee were able to link together. He also ordered Sedgwick to immediately attack at Fredericksburg. Up until this time, Early had succeeded in holding off far greater Union numbers there.

On May 3, thousands of Confederates assaulted the Union line around Chancellorsville with great loss. Finally, the Union line broke (Hooker himself was knocked unconscious when a cannonball struck a pillar of the mansion and debris struck him in the head; he was out of commission for the next three hours) and Hooker's men fell back to their prepared interior line. At 10:00 A.M. Lee met Stuart near what remained of the Chancellor mansion. Stuart had done a commendable job in taking over for Jackson.

Lee was planning on renewing the attack on Hooker's next line when he received word that Sedgwick had finally broken through the Confederate line at Fredericksburg. With these troops now approaching his rear, Lee had no choice but to turn his attention momentarily east-ward. He split his forces for a third time during the campaign, dispatching troops under Lafayette McLaws to help Early and Wilcox (who had brought his men down from Banks's Ford to help Early) fight Sedgwick. On the afternoon of May 3, the Confederates fought a sharp fight with Sedgwick's Federals at Salem Church, a few miles west of Fredericksburg. By evening, they had managed to turn Sedgwick back.

On May 4, Lee was anxious to keep the pressure on Hooker and was contemplating how to assault the new Union position. He realized that he needed to use all his men for such an attack to have a chance to succeed, and with Sedgwick still at his rear this was impossible. So out of necessity Lee focused again on Sedgwick by instructing his generals to attack, envelop, and destroy him. But Sedgwick had regrouped into a strong rectangular formation north of the Plank Road, and it was not until dusk that the Confederates completed their reconnaissance and made their attack. The attack drove Sedgwick back to the banks of the Rappahannock, but darkness prevented Lee from finishing him off. All the while, Hooker's troops sat quietly within their lines at Chancellorsville.

During all this time, Brigadier General George Stoneman's Union cavalry, which was wreaking havoc just north of Richmond, had no effect on the events at Chancellorsville. After Lee had won, the cavalry units made their way back to northern Virginia.

On the morning of May 5, Lee was disappointed to learn that Sedgwick had successfully crossed back over the river during the night. While frustrated at the escape, this meant that Lee could now concentrate on Hooker's main position. It would be a formidable task. Hooker had over 90,000 men (compared to 35,000 for Lee) concentrated along five miles of breastworks, dug and refortified for two days.[25] It was possibly the strongest field position developed by either side during the entire war.

Still, Lee had supreme confidence in his men and began working on the logistics for the assault. Without much artillery support, ruled out by the Wilderness, things would be even tougher for the Confederates. Probably only one other man on the field had confidence that Lee could somehow take the Union position and that was Joe Hooker. If Hooker had been planning on making a stand south of the river, a fierce

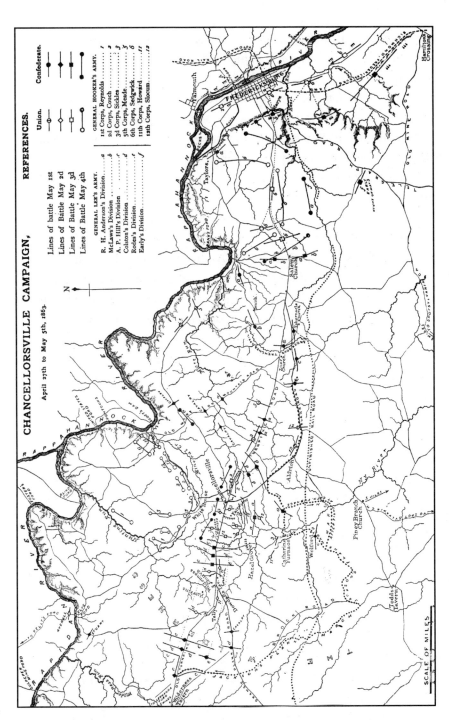

Fig. 8.5. The Chancellorsville Campaign

Battles and Leaders of the Civil War

rainstorm on the afternoon and early evening of May 5 must have changed his mind. With the Rappahannock rising and his bridges becoming more and more unstable, Hooker decided to take his force back across the river. When Lee's pickets moved forward on the morning of May 6, they were amazed to find the entire Union position deserted.

It was Robert E. Lee's greatest moment. Outnumbered more than two to one, he had consistently made daring moves to embarrass Hooker and had driven the Army of the Potomac once again back in shameful retreat. The South rejoiced.

Chancellorsville was probably also the high point in Confederate military history. It also served as a prelude to the next great conflict in the East, at Gettysburg, in July 1863. As in the spring, Lee who was faced that summer with finding food and forage decided to take his men to the fertile fields of Pennsylvania. But Chancellorsville had taken its toll. The brutal fighting there had robbed him of many good men and many fine officers in addition to Stonewall Jackson. Faulty command decisions by men new to their rank would haunt the Confederates at Gettysburg.

Lee himself was also affected in a negative way by his victory at Chancellorsville. After the crushing defeat of the Union army at Fredericksburg in December and his masterful chess game at Chancellorsville, Lee had become overconfident in his men and possibly in himself. The victory at Chancellorsville must have had some role in Lee's decision to send a wave of men to their doom in the Gettysburg charge of July 3, 1863.

What if the acoustic shadow at Chancellorsville had not occurred? What if Hooker had heard Jackson's attack as soon as it began? It seems likely that the battle would have been drastically different, because Hooker would probably have been able to stem the tide of the Confederate onslaught farther to the west than where it actually was stopped. On May 3, Hooker pulled Sickles (with two divisions and a considerable amount of artillery) from the Hazel Grove plateau back towards Chancellorsville because he felt that Sickles was too isolated in that position. If Hooker had been alerted to Jackson's attack and stopped it farther down the Orange Turnpike, he would probably have held onto Hazel Grove.

As it turned out, Hazel Grove was the key to the position of May 3, as the Confederates filled the plateau with artillery and battered the Union first line around the Chancellor mansion. If Hooker had held onto the position, it is doubtful that Stuart and Lee would have been able to join forces. Perhaps Hooker would have regrouped behind his fortifications and gone back on the attack.

Chancellorsville was a complicated series of small battles, and the acoustic shadow west of the Chancellor mansion added to the chaos. As at Seven Pines, Robert E. Lee was given an inadvertent career boost by the unusual behavior of sound in the atmosphere. Two years later, he would finally have acoustics work against him at Five Forks.

Chapter 9

Five Forks, Virginia

An acoustic shadow at Seven Pines helped bring Robert E. Lee to prominence. What may have been an acoustic shadow at Five Forks helped bring his military career to a close.

Background

By March 1865, the Confederacy was a shadow of what it had been in its glory days of 1862. Long gone were hopes of intervention by the British or French, and probably very few of the men in butternut actually held hopes of winning the war. It had become a thing of determination only, a mutual decision among the small band of men remaining to hold on until the end, however it came.

The capture of Vicksburg in July 1863 had opened the Mississippi River and isolated the parts of the Confederacy west of the river. Forces under Major General William T. Sherman had driven all the way from Chattanooga to the Atlantic shore and were now working their way up through North Carolina.

In Virginia, Robert E. Lee had finally been cornered. Union troops under Lieutenant General Ulysses S. Grant and Major General George Meade had traded blows with the Army of Northern Virginia from the Wilderness, through Spotsylvania and Cold Harbor, to Petersburg. There, in June of 1864, both armies dug in for what proved to be an exhausting siege.

By March of 1865, the Union army had stretched Lee's army to the breaking point. The left flank of the Confederate line was at the Nine Mile Road, near the battlefield of Seven Pines, where eighteen hundred cavalry troopers under Major General Fitzhugh Lee guarded the Chickahominy River crossings. The line of fortifications ran across the James and down to Petersburg and then ran west. The right flank was manned by a small corps (one infantry division and one artillery division) commanded by Lieutenant General Richard Anderson, and was located about 10 miles west of Petersburg. The entire line was a little more than 27 miles long and Lee was able to place an average of only a little over a thousand men per mile.[1]

Fig. 9.1. Ulysses S. Grant in 1865

National Archives

With only one man every five feet or so, Lee did not have many options for shuffling troops from point to point. The only reserve was a division under Major General George Pickett, whose five thousand men were scattered behind the line at various points. The division had not seen much action since suffering devastating losses during the charge on the third day of fighting at Gettysburg in 1863.

As winter turned to spring, men on both sides knew that major fighting looked imminent. As often happened in the war, Lee was able to guess his opponent's plan. Unfortunately for Lee, there was not much he could do about it. Although Grant did not mind sending his men against enemy fortifications, Lee correctly predicted that this time Grant would try for a turning movement on the Confederate right flank. This flank was "up in the air" and had no cavalry to warn of an impending attack. More importantly, an attack on this end would allow the Union army to cut the all-important Southside Railroad, one of only two routes by which food and provisions could be supplied to Lee's weary and hungry men.

On March 27, Lee received information from Confederate scouts that the Union cavalry north of the James River (about nine thousand men under Major General Philip Sheridan) had moved out in great haste. This movement could have been in preparation for Sheridan joining Sherman in wiping out the Confederates remaining in North Carolina, but it was more likely the beginning of the expected turning movement on Lee's right flank. Since Lee could not extend his weakened lines any farther, his best hope was to use any available men to strike Sheridan before Sheridan could get on his flank. With the advice of Major General James Longstreet, Lee decided to assemble a mobile task force to go after Sheridan and protect the right flank.

Fig. 9.2. George Pickett
Library of Congress

By the twenty-ninth, the task force was beginning to come together. Pickett's five thousand men were moved by trains to Sutherland Station, 10 miles west of Petersburg. From there, they would march toward Five Forks, a country intersection of four roads a couple of miles south of the railroad. Here the White Oak Road ran from east to west, Scott's Road came in from the southwest, Ford's Road ran north from the intersection, and the Courthouse Road came in from the southeast. Because the White Oak Road continues through the intersection (instead of terminating like the other three roads), the intersection has the appearance of a five-sided star.

It was at Five Forks that Lee thought Sheridan would gather his troopers before attacking the railroad. Joining Pickett would be Fitzhugh Lee's cavalry (about eighteen hundred troopers), pulled from the left flank, and additional cavalry under Major General William "Rooney" Lee (twenty-four hundred men) and Major General Thomas Rosser. Rosser's twelve hundred men had just arrived from the Shenandoah Valley, where they had seen hard fighting.[2]

Grant's plan called for Sheridan to move quickly behind the Union infantry and head towards Dinwiddie Court House. Once there, Sheridan was to make for the Southside Railroad and the Richmond and Danville Railroad and wreck them. He was to attack any Confederates who left the safety of their fortifications to get in his way. To aid Sheridan, two Union infantry corps, the II (under Major General Andrew Humphreys) and the V (under Major General Gouverneur Warren) would move towards the Confederate right flank and be prepared to attack as events dictated. Both infantry corps would travel light, with very little artillery.[3] Artillery would not have been of much help in the densely wooded country west of Petersburg anyway. If the Confederates shifted men from the Petersburg line toward the right flank, the Union troops at Petersburg would immediately attack.

On the twenty-ninth, advance units of the Union II and V Corps made contact with small detachments of Confederates west of Petersburg. After some lively fighting, the Union troops pushed the Confederate outposts back toward Anderson's main detachment. Both sides encountered trouble with deployment of their men due to the tangled underbrush and swampy conditions.[4] When Lee learned that Union infantry would be aiding Sheridan in the turning movement, he ordered a 21-gun artillery battalion under Colonel William Pegram to move to the right flank.[5]

On March 31, a larger battle occurred, this time at Dinwiddie Court House. Sheridan, who had moved rapidly behind Warren's V Corps, ran into a wall when Confederate cavalry under Fitzhugh Lee and several of Pickett's infantry brigades attacked him. Though Sheridan steadied his retreating men and established a line near Dinwiddie Court House by dark, the attack had certainly taken the initiative from the Union cavalry. Still, Sheridan was not discouraged, knowing that he had two infantry corps at his disposal to the north. Speaking of Pickett's men, Sheridan said:

> This force is in more danger than I am—if I am cut off from
> the Army of the Potomac, it is cut off from Lee's army, and not a
> man in it should ever be allowed to get back to Lee. We at last
> have drawn the enemy's infantry out of it fortifications, and this is
> our chance to attack it.[6]

There had also been fighting to the north that day, when Anderson's men (led by Major General Bushrod Johnson) had attacked Humphrey's II corps. After some initial gains, the Confederates had been thrown back. More importantly, they lost control of the White Oak Road that directly connected Anderson's position with Five Forks.

Late on the night of the thirty-first, Pickett received word of Johnson's loss and of advances by Warren's V Corps north of him. In light of this information, Pickett decided that it would be unwise to hold his current position at Dinwiddie Court House, fearing that Warren and Sheridan might trap him. Before dawn on April 1, the Confederates began to move back towards Five Forks.

That morning Pickett received a telegram from Lee: "Hold Five Forks at all hazards. Protect road from Ford's Depot and prevent Union forces from striking the Southside Railroad. Regret exceedingly your forced withdrawal, and your inability to hold the advantage you had gained."[7]

Though Pickett would have been more comfortable setting up a defensive position a couple of miles north of Five Forks, on the north bank of Hatcher's Run, Lee was correct in asserting that Five Forks must be defended. Although the position offered little in the way of natural defensive possibilities, if the Union held the intersection they would easily be able to move westward on White Oak Road and turn the Confederate line.

While Sheridan's troopers maintained contact with the Confederates during the retreat, Pickett seems not to have expected an attack on April 1. It is also likely that both Pickett and Fitzhugh Lee expected that men from Anderson's position would soon reinforce them.[8] In any event, the Confederates at Five Forks did throw up some cursory breastworks of logs and dirt along the north side of the White Oak Road and then fell down exhausted. In the words of Fitzhugh Lee:

> When we moved towards Five Forks, hearing nothing more of...(Warren's) infantry's move which we had heard of the night before, I thought that the movements just there, for the time being, were suspended, and we were not expecting any attack that afternoon, so far as I know. Our throwing up works and taking positions were simply general matters of military precaution.[9]

Pickett placed Rooney Lee's cavalry division on his right and the 8th Virginia Cavalry under Colonel Thomas Munford on his left flank. The main line of defense consisted of five infantry brigades posted along the White Oak Road, with the left end of the fortifications "refused" at a 90-degree angle for about one hundred fifty yards to the north.[10] The brigades were commanded by (running from left flank to right flank) Brigadier Generals Matt Ransom, William Wallace, and George Steuart, Colonel Joseph Mayo (filling in for William Terry, wounded at Dinwiddie Court House), and Montgomery Corse, another brigadier. The line was a little less than two miles in length.[11] Pickett had 10 guns at his disposal. He placed three on the right, three near the Five Forks intersection, and the other four on the left flank. Pickett sent Rosser and his men about a mile and a half north of Five Forks to the north side of Hatcher's Run. Here they would guard the Confederate wagon train.

After settling in at Hatcher's Run, Rosser sent an invitation for lunch to Pickett and Fitzhugh Lee. A couple of days earlier, while stationed near the Nottoway River, Rosser had borrowed a fishing seine from a farmer and gathered a large number of shad. After consuming some of the fish that day, he had plenty to bring with him when ordered to join Pickett. Even in modern times, shad "bakes" (at which the fish are actually broiled over open fires) are a tradition in eastern Virginia during the spring, when the shad leave their coastal homes and travel far up coastal rivers to spawn. The hot flames of a shad bake help to disintegrate the fish's many tiny bones. Now that there appeared to be a respite in the fighting, Rosser figured that it would be a good time to share his find with his fellow generals.

At this point in the war, most of the Confederates were hungry, even those wearing stars. Pickett's artillerists had been driven to eating the corn meant for their horses. Rosser's invitation must have been too good to pass up. In any event, at some point in the early afternoon, both Fitzhugh Lee and Pickett left the front lines to join Rosser at Hatcher's Run. Inexcusably, they did not tell their subordinates that they were leaving, perhaps due to shame at the feast they were about to enjoy.

As Fitz Lee was preparing to leave, Munford rode up with the news that Union cavalry was attacking the far left of the Confederate position at Five Forks. Not expecting a major attack at this time, and most likely anxious to get to the shad bake, Lee replied: "Well, Munford, I wish you would go over in person at once and see what this means and, if necessary, order up your Division and let me hear from you."

The action on the Confederate left signaled more than a cavalry skirmish. The hard-driving Sheridan was pushing his men hard and a full-scale attack on the Five Forks position was coming soon.

The Battle and the Acoustics

Sheridan's plan called for the infantry under Warren (about 12,000 men ready for duty at this point) to strike at the Confederate left, near the refused angle. The dismounted (due to the thick woods) Union cavalry would then strike at the Confederate right and center when the sounds of Warren's attack were heard.

Warren received his orders at about 1:00 P.M., and it was about 4:15 P.M. when his men began their attack.[12] It was a beautiful, sunny day (following several days of dreary rain) and Warren instructed his men to "keep closed to the left and to preserve their direction in the woods, by keeping the sun, then shining brightly, in the same position over their left shoulders."[13]

As the entire Union V Corps moved towards his cavalry, posted in front of the refused angle, Munford frantically sent messengers to Fitz Lee and Pickett. No one knew where they were. As the Union infantry men closed on the angle, Sheridan, riding in their midst, shouted: "Go at 'em with a will! Move on at a clean jump or you'll not catch one of them. They're all getting ready to run now, and if you don't get them in five minutes, they'll every one of them get away from you! Now go for them!"[14]

Sheridan was not far off in his assessment. The Confederate resistance at the angle crumbled quickly. As the Yankees approached, the four Confederate guns on the left were limbered off and rushed toward Ford's Road. Thousands of Confederates were quickly captured, while the rest were either shot or fled through the woods towards Ford's Road. Sheridan jumped his horse Rienzi over the angle and landed in the midst of a group of prisoners. Pointing over his shoulder to the rear, he told them: "Get right along, now. Drop your guns; you'll never need them

Fig. 9.3. Fitzhugh Lee

Library of Congress

Fig. 9.4. Philip Sheridan

National Archives

Fig. 9.5. Thomas Rosser

United States Military History Institute

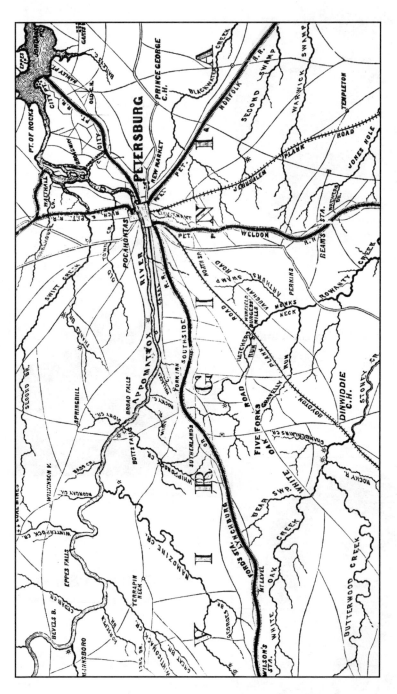

Fig. 9.6. The Five Forks Region

Draper, *History of the American Civil War*

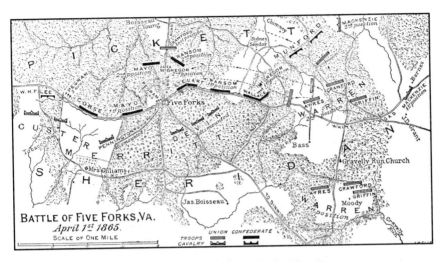

Fig. 9.7. The Battle of Five Forks

Battles and Leaders of the Civil War

anymore. You'll all be safe over there. Are there any more of you? We want every one of you fellows."

The retreat of the Confederates at the angle now exposed the flank of Wallace's position. Wallace's brigade and the remnants of Ransom's command fell back to Steuart's left flank and began to quickly attempt to build a new line of works perpendicular to what remained of the main line. As the Union troops advanced, the fighting at this new line was fierce. The Confederates, fighting hand-to-hand, must have sensed that the fate of the Confederacy rested on them. Finally, the greater Union numbers broke the Confederate line and the remaining men of Wallace's and Ransom's brigades retreated toward Ford's Road.

Meanwhile, the rest of the Confederate line along the White Oak Road was being hard pressed by the Union cavalry. When the men of the V Corps reached Ford's Road, Warren ordered them to head south and take the Confederate position along White Oak Road from the rear.

So where were Pickett and Fitz Lee while their entire position was disintegrating? Apparently, they continued to enjoy their shad (and perhaps some alcohol as well) late into the afternoon, oblivious to the disaster around them. At one point during the feast, two pickets dashed up to inform the generals that the Yankees were advancing on them all along the front. According to Rosser:

These reports were made to Pickett and to Lee and the position at Five Forks was considered as well chosen and strong but little attention was given to the enemy's advance. I was suffering from my wound and as I was not immediately in command of the pickets I took no steps to reinforce them. Indeed the pickets were a part of...Munford's command and I, reporting direct to General Lee, and as he was present, felt little or no concern about them.

How could the generals sit, unconcerned, in the midst of such an attack? Apparently because little or no sound from the attack managed to reach their ears. Not expecting an attack, they must have felt that the reports reaching them were merely an overreaction by their troops to some minor skirmishing.

Finally, later in the afternoon, Pickett requested that Rosser send a courier down to Five Forks to find out what, if anything, was happening. Rosser had a habit of sending two couriers, separated but within sight of each other. As the generals resumed their sociable conversation, there was a burst of gunfire from the south side of Hatcher's Run. To their horror, the generals watched the lead courier be taken prisoner by an advancing wave of men in blue. In almost total ignorance of the attack, here was the Union V Corps breaking onto the Ford's Road, between the generals and their men.

Pickett jumped onto a horse and galloped across Hatcher's Run. He yelled at the Confederates who were still attempting resistance there to hold the Union forces until he could reach Five Forks. A brave charge by the 2nd Virginia Cavalry gave him enough time. Leaning to the far side of his horse, Pickett dashed through the gap and made his way to Five Forks. It was too late for Lee to run the gauntlet; he quickly helped Rosser form his men north of Hatcher's Run to protect the railroad.

When Pickett reached Five Forks he could begin to see the extent of the disaster. While trying to hold together what remained of the Confederate line along the White Oak Road, he ordered most of Mayo's brigade back up Ford's Road to deal with the Yankees approaching from the rear. The overwhelming Union numbers soon pushed Mayo's men out of the way, those not captured or shot making their way through the woods to the northwest.

This left the troops under Corse and Rooney Lee on the far right, who had, up to this point, held their own against the attacking Union cavalrymen. Now with Union troops attacking them from east, west, and south, they reformed their lines as best they could, but they were soon overwhelmed. As darkness covered the field, the entire Confederate line collapsed and those who could made their way north through the woods to the Southside Railroad.

Sheridan's men had achieved a complete victory. The right flank of the Confederate line surrounding Petersburg was now open to him, as was the Southside Railroad. With the help of surprise, superior numbers and, possibly, some unusual acoustics, he had helped bring the Confederacy to its knees.

Did an acoustic shadow occur at Five Forks? If so, what could have caused it? Many secondhand accounts of the battle mention the acoustic shadow as fact.[15] Union General Humphreys, who was in the vicinity, though not at the scene, wrote later: "A singular circumstance connected with this battle is the fact that Gen. Pickett was, all of this time and until near the close of the action, on the north side of Hatchers Run where he heard no sound of the engagement, nor had he received any information concerning it."

Though Pickett does not appear to have commented in writing on the acoustic shadow, both Rosser and Fitzhugh Lee mentioned it years later. Rosser stated: "Some time was spent over the lunch, during which no firing was heard. And we concluded that the enemy was not in much of a hurry to find us a Five Forks."[16]

Lee also states that those at the fish bake heard little of the battle. After the war, during a court of inquiry in the case of Gouverneur Warren (removed from command after the battle by Grant and Sheridan due to what they perceived as tardiness in his troop movements), Lee was asked a series of questions about the battle. What follows is an excerpt of the portion of the inquiry transcript relating to the acoustics of the battle (the first question refers to the time period between the beginning of the attack and the arrival of the Union troops at Ford's Road):

Q. During that time how much firing did you hear?

A. I did not hear a shot.

Q. Was the whole country south of Hatcher's Run thickly wooded?

A. My recollection is that is was thickly wooded—a great many bushes—my experience is that in certain conditions of the atmosphere, and in certain tracts of woodland, it is very difficult to the hear the firing of infantry. You can only hear the firing of infantry at a short distance when the undergrowth is thick.

Q. You say until you got at the ford you did not hear any?

A. I did not hear any. General Pickett, who was closer than I, for he was justalong the run, evidently did not hear it either, for he only got across this ford just about the time the Federal infantry got possession of that road. As I reached the ford upon the north side, he had crossed it and was on the south side. I saw him throw himself on his saddle, as I said before, and saw that he was being shot at. When I got to the ford, I could not cross it.[17]

There was controversy for years regarding the events at Five Forks. Neither Pickett nor Fitzhugh Lee (understandably) mentioned the shad bake in their official reports, and it was not until more than 20 years after the war that Rosser finally told the story.[18] One might at first think that Lee's story of being caught in an acoustic shadow was an attempt at justifying his lack of action in the battle. The confirmation by Rosser, however, who had come clean about his role in the lunch, bears out the reality of the acoustic shadow.

Before looking at the possible physical causes for the acoustic shadow, one might ponder other, more human factors. The generals were finally getting a chance to relax, with good food and fellowship, after days, months, and years of hardship. None appears to have thought an attack to be imminent, a view that may have helped them attribute any muffled sounds of battle to skirmishing. And finally, alcohol may have had some effect, though none of the generals mention passing a bottle. For years in the South, allegations of drunkenness were whispered when Five Forks was discussed. Though there is no confirmation of inebriation, if some alcohol was consumed around the fire it would certainly have made the generals more relaxed and less alert.

One of Munford's couriers apparently did make it through to the generals during the course of the afternoon. According to J. B. Flippin, a sergeant in the 3rd Virginia Cavalry, writing to Munford: "I found Genl Fitz Lee & Pickett sitting under a fly tent – at least 2 miles in your rear, with a bottle of whiskey or Brandy. I don't know which for I was not invited to partake of it. I delivered your message & he told me to tell you to do the best you could. I remember full well that you looked much disappointed at the order I brought you."[19]

Physically, it is very unlikely that the weather played a major role in the acoustics at Five Forks. It had rained on Thursday, March 30, and until noon on Friday, March 31, but Saturday, April 1, was sunny and pleasant.[20] The rain may have lingered on the foliage, however, and intensified any damping of sound that occurred. There are no indications that there was significant wind in any direction at Five Forks on that day.

It is much more likely that Lee and Pickett were the victims of substantial attenuation of sound due to interaction of the sound waves with the dense foliage. As in several other battles reviewed in this book, the woods were thick and filled with undergrowth. Both infantry and cavalry had trouble making any type of maneuver. One Union officer described it in these words: "It is a section of country more difficult for cavalry operations than it is possible to imagine: the fields all quicksands, the woods all jungle..."[21]

Union Brevet Major General Samuel W. Crawford, whose troops were part of the V Corps attack, described the region as consisting of "...bogs, tangled woods, and thickets of pine, interspersed with open spaces here and there."[22] Colonel Thomas McCoy, whose 107th Pennsylvania also took part in the assault, said: "The ground over which we were to pass was composed of woods, fields, thickets of underbrush, swamps, ditches, streams, etc."[23] It was surely the sort of countryside in which one would expect sound to have a tough time carrying very far. Though the ground was generally flat, many ditches and ravines cut through it. These could hinder any sound waves propagating along the ground.

Adding to the likelihood that sounds of the battle did not carry well to the site of the shad bake was the lack of artillery in the battle. There was no Union artillery used in the battle at all and almost half of the 10 Confederate guns were withdrawn from action at the refused angle as soon as the attack began. The higher frequency, smaller sound waves produced by musketry would be much more likely to have been strongly absorbed and scattered by the trees and underbrush.

One odd aspect of all this is that on the day of the battle and in the days leading up to it, sounds apparently carried well enough through the forest to be heard by others. For example, the Union cavalrymen along White Oak Road were to begin attacking when they heard sounds of the initial assault by the V Corps a mile down the road. According to Sheridan: "...the firing of the 5th Corps was the signal for General (Wesley) Merritt to assault, which was promptly responded to."[24] Brevet Major General George Custer, also along the White Oak Road, said, describing the timing for his men to begin action: "As soon as the firing on the line held by the V Corps indicated the inauguration of the attack..."[25]

In the days just before the battle, Union scouts at Five Forks heard the trains of the Southside Railroad three miles to the north, well enough to note their direction.[26] At the battle of Dinwiddie Court House, the sounds of Pickett's guns were successfully used as a signal to Munford's men to attack.[27] In that same battle, Union cavalry were alerted to the Confederate attack by the sounds of firing some miles away.[28] Warren's troops, not involved in the battle, clearly heard the sounds of the fight to their southwest.[29] The infantry battle at Anderson's position near the White Oak Road, also on March 31, was audible all the way to Meade's headquarters near Petersburg.[30] There are also accounts stating that the Five Forks battle was audible at Anderson's headquarters, several miles to the east.[31]

Though the fighting at Five Forks was almost all musketry, the amount of noise generated must have been considerable. According to Warren, commanding the V Corps, the firing was heavy.[32] A description of the attack by the Union cavalry along the White Oak Road included the following reference to the sounds of their repeating rifles: "Those who had magazine guns created a racket in those pine woods that sounded as if a couple of army corps had opened fire."[33] Another account speaks of the "dreadful roar of musketry"[34] and "great shocks of musketry thundering back and forth through the dark woods."[35]

So it seems certain that the sounds of battle could carry through the countryside around Five Forks. Perhaps the White Oak Road acted as some sort of acoustic corridor, aiding in the transport of sounds on an east-west axis but not in the perpendicular direction. But why then didn't Ford's Road carry some of the sounds of the battle northward to Pickett and Lee? Indeed, most of the artillery used in the battle was located near where Ford's Road intersects the White Oak Road and it was still in use after Pickett had become aware of the battle.[36]

When Warren reached the Ford's Road, he directed the infantry to move towards the sounds of firing coming from the southwest (where Rooney Lee was holding off the Union cavalry). How could Pickett and Lee not have heard firing when they were just a bit farther down the same road? It may be that in a forest this dense, being three-quarters of a mile from the front (as was Warren) offered significantly better acoustics than being twice that distance (as were Pickett and Lee). Those sounds that were able to make their way above the forest may have been transported without difficulty several miles away (to Anderson or Meade, for example). There was a bend in Ford's Road in between Warren's position and that of the two Confederate generals, and this may also have played some role in keeping the latter in silence.

In summary, it appears that Pickett and Lee were in an acoustic shadow partially of their own making and partially due to physical factors. Overconfidence, exhaustion, alcohol, and the absorption of sounds by the surrounding foliage combined to keep the generals unaware of the desperate fighting all around them.

The Aftermath

The total number of Confederates killed, captured, and wounded at Five Forks probably numbered about one-third of the nine thousand men who began the fight. The strategic losses were much greater.

At about 5:45 P.M., Robert E. Lee first learned preliminary news of the rout. His first reaction was to order three of Bushrod Johnson's brigades to the Southside Railroad where Ford's Road crossed it. This essentially emptied the trenches where Anderson had been protecting the right flank of the Petersburg fortifications.

Later that evening, Grant learned of the victory. After asking for a report on the number of prisoners, he walked to the telegraph tent. Returning to the group of officers with which he had been talking, he remarked, "I have ordered an immediate assault along the lines."[37]

This was truly the beginning of the end. Lee, knowing the entire Confederate position was now untenable, sent a message to Jefferson Davis, informing him that the army was pulling out to the north side of the Appomattox River, and was heading for Amelia Court House. By getting around Sheridan, Lee hoped to be able to receive supplies heading down the Southside Railroad from Lynchburg, and to possibly escape southwest to join Johnston's army in North Carolina. Lee's hopes were not fulfilled, as Sheridan and the remaining Union army joined in a furious pursuit that ended a week later at Appomattox Court House.

Five Forks is often referred to as "The Waterloo of the Confederacy." Even without the surprise caused by the acoustics, there is certainly no guarantee that Pickett would have been able to hold Five Forks against Sheridan's onslaught. But it is likely that the Confederates would have made a better showing than the rout that occurred, and maybe held out long enough for Lee to reinforce the position.

The reality of what happened at Five Forks lingered for years as a low point in the collective Southern memory. One former Confederate officer, writing to Thomas Munford, stated: "I think you are mistaken in the opinion that the Battle of Five Forks is not generally understood by the survivors of the Army of Northern Virginia. The shad lunch, the whiskey, and the sad catastrophe to the Army of Northern Virginia, of which they were the prime factors—were well known & deplored at the time & they are remembered today with keen regret. I wish they could be obliterated from our Confederate annals. Five Forks is the chief blot upon the otherwise fair and glorious record of Gen. Lee's army."[38]

And Jefferson Davis, writing years after the war to Munford: "…it was hardly exaggerated when you speak of that fatal lunch as the ruin of the Confederacy. It certainly did at least hasten the catastrophe."[39]

While these comments go a bit too far in placing the blame on the Five Forks disaster for what was probably the inevitable end of the Confederacy, the loss was a large factor in bringing about the end of Lee's army. It is interesting to see that Lee's career at the head of the Army of Northern Virginia was framed at one end by the acoustics at Seven Pines and on the other end by the acoustics at Five Forks.

Notes

CHAPTER 1

1. Douglas Southall Freeman, *Lee's Lieutenants: A Study in Command* (New York: C. Scribner's Sons, 1943), 531.
2. Robert Underwood Johnson and Clarence Clough Buel, eds., *Battles and Leaders of the Civil War*, 4 vols. (New York: T. Yoseloff, 1956), vol. 4, 337. (Hereafter cited as *Battles and Leaders*.)
3. E. P. Alexander, *Military Memoirs of a Confederate* (New York: C. Scribner's Sons, 1907), 127.
4. Heros von Borcke, *Memoirs of the Confederate War* (New York: Peter Smith, 1938), 55.
5. John Tyndall, *Sound* (New York: D. Appleton and Company, 1896), 304–6.
6. Stephen W. Sears, *To the Gates of Richmond: The Peninsula Campaign* (New York: Ticknor and Fields, 1992), 222.
7. *Battles and Leaders*, vol. 2, 365.
8. Freeman, *Lee's Lieutenants*, 531.

CHAPTER 2

1. Harry F. Olson, *Music, Physics and Engineering* (New York: Dover Publications, Inc., 1967), 3.
2. In reality, even a reed or tuning fork produces a sound that is more complex than the simple one-frequency pure tone described in the text.
3. Dr. G. Richard Price, U.S. Army Human Engineering Laboratory, personal communication.
4. Sir James Jeans, *Science and Music* (New York: Dover Publications, Inc., 1968), 120. The formal equation for determining the speed of sound in dry air is Laplace's formula:

$$c = (\gamma R_0 T/M)^{0.5}$$

where c is the speed of sound, T is the absolute temperature in Kelvins, R_0 is the universal gas constant (8314 J kg^{-1} K^{-1}), M is the average molecular weight of the air and γ is the specific heat ratio. When expanded as a MacLaurin series in T, one has for the speed in m/s and the temperature in degree Celsius:

$$c(m/s) = 331.36 + 0.6067T$$

5. George R. Garinther, Joel T. Kalb, David C. Hodge, and G. Richard Price, *Proposed Aural Nondectability Limits for Army Materiel* (Aberdeen Proving Ground, Maryland: U.S. Army Human Engineering Laboratory, Technical Memorandum 3–85, March 1985), 13.
6. Ibid., 13.
7. Ibid., 18.
8. Ibid., 25.
9. Ibid., 26.
10. Clyde Orr, Jr., *Between Earth and Space* (New York: Macmillan, 1960), 123.
11. Ibid., 126.
12. This means that outdoor sounds are normally heard better at night than during the daytime. This nighttime audibility is also enhanced by a decrease in ambient noise. Even in Civil War times, ambient noise would decrease at night because generally lower winds would mean less rustling of leaves, etc.

161

13. *Battles and Leaders*, vol. 1, 713.

14. Robert G. Fleagle and Joost A. Businger, *An Introduction to Atmospheric Physics* (New York: Academic Press, 1963), 293.

15. *Battles and Leaders*, vol. 2, 365.

16. Robert Latham, ed., *The Shorter Pepys* (London: Bell and Hyman, 1985), 625.

17. Cicely M. Botley, "Abnormal Audibility," *Weather*, 21 (1966): 232.

18. Robert T. Beyer, *Sounds of Our Times* (New York: Springer-Verlag, 1999), 6.

19. E. H. Brown and F. F. Hall, Jr., "Advances in Atmospheric Acoustics," *Rev. Geophys. Space Phys.*, 16 (1978), 47.

20. John Tyndall, *Sound* (New York: D. Appleton and Company, 1896), 289.

21. Ibid., 321.

22. Clifton Fadiman, introduction to *The Collected Writings of Ambrose Bierce* (New York: Citadel Press, 1946), 470.

23. Beyer, *Sounds of Our Times*, 195.

24. Orr, Jr., *Between Earth and Space*, 127.

25. John Albright, *Physical Meteorology* (New York: Prentice-Hall, Inc., 1939), 346.

26. Beyer, *Sounds of Our Times*, 195.

27. Fleagle and Businger, *An Introduction to Atmospheric Physics*, 292.

28. Albright, *Physical Meteorology*, 347.

29. Orr, Jr., *Between Earth and Space*, 128.

30. Ibid., 129.

CHAPTER 3

1. E. P. Alexander, *Military Memoirs of a Confederate* (New York: C. Scribner's Sons, 1907), 30.

2. Ibid., 34.

3. Tom D. Crouch, *The Eagle Aloft* (Washington: Smithsonian Press, 1983), 391.

4. Alexander, *Military Memoirs of a Confederate*, 32.

5. Ibid., 33.

6. Ibid., 35.

7. Ibid., 34.

8. Ibid., 129.

9. Ibid., 139.

CHAPTER 4

1. Bruce Catton, *Grant Moves South* (Boston: Little, Brown and Company, 1960), 110.

2. M. F. Force, *From Fort Henry to Corinth* (Wilmington, North Carolina: Broadfoot Publishing Company, 1989), ii.

3. Catton, *Grant Moves South*, 130.

4. *War of the Rebellion: A Compilation of the Official Records of the Union and Confederate Armies* (Washington: Government Printing Office, 1880–1901), ser. 1, vol. 7, pt. 1, 139. (Hereafter cited as *Official Records.*)

5. Ibid., 124.

6. Spencer C. Tucker, *Andrew Foote: Civil War Admiral on Western Waters* (Annapolis: Naval Institute Press, 2000), 147.

7. Benjamin Cooling, *Forts Henry and Donelson: The Key to the Confederate Heartland* (Knoxville: The University of Tennessee Press, 1987), 126.

8. Tucker, *Andrew Foote*, 149.

9. Force, *From Fort Henry to Corinth*, 39.

10. *New York Herald*, February 21, 1862.

11. *Official Records,* ser. 1, vol. 7, pt. 1, 175.

12. Cooling, *Forts Henry and Donelson*, 175.

13. John S. C. Abbott, *The Life of General Ulysses S. Grant* (Boston: B. B. Russell, 1868), 53.

14. William Taylor Adams, *Our Standard Bearer* (Boston: Lee and Shepard, 1888), 146.

15. Force, *From Fort Henry to Corinth*, 48.

16. Shelby Foote, *The Civil War – A Narrative*, 3 vols. (New York: Random House, 1963) vol. 1, 207.

17. *Official Records*, ser. 1, vol. 7, pt. 1, 237.

18. Ibid.

19. Ibid., 186, 199, 209, 216, 252.

20. Ibid., 174, 185, 194.

21. Abbott, *The Life of General Ulysses S. Grant,* 53; Cooling, *Forts Henry and Donelson*, 200.

22. *Official Records*, ser. 1, vol. 7, pt. 1, 266, 356.

23. Ibid., 162, 356.

24. *Battles and Leaders*, vol. 1, 415.

25. *Official Records*, ser. 1, vol. 7, pt. 1, 161.

CHAPTER 5

1. Richard Wheeler, *Sword Over Richmond* (New York: Harper and Row, 1986), 64.

2. *Battles and Leaders*, vol. 2, 211.

3. Ibid., 226.

4. Ibid.

5. Steven H. Newton, *The Battle of Seven Pines* (Lynchburg, Virginia: H. E. Howard, Inc. 1993), 71.

6. E. P. Alexander, *Military Memoirs of a Confederate* (New York: Charles Scribner's Sons, 1907), 81.

7. Newton, *The Battle of Seven Pines*, 62.

8. *Official Records*, ser. 1, vol. 11, pt. 1, 934.

9. *Battles and Leaders*, vol. 2, 213.

10. Ibid., 244.

11. Douglas Southall Freeman, *Lee's Lieutenants: A Study in Command*, 3 vols. (New York: Charles Scribner's Sons, 1944), vol. 1, 237.

12. Newton, *The Battle of Seven Pines*, 71.

13. Jefferson Davis, *The Rise and Fall of the Confederate Government*, 2 vols. (New York: D. Appleton and Co., 1881), vol. 2, 122.

14. *Official Records*, ser. 1, vol. 11, pt. 1, 775.

15. Ibid., 782.

16. Ibid., 802.

17. Ibid., 807.

18. Wheeler, *Sword Over Richmond*, 228.

19. *Battles and Leaders*, vol. 2, 238.

20. *Official Records*, ser. 1, vol. 11, pt. 1, 813.

21. Ibid., 879.

22. Ibid., 892.

23. Ibid., 909.

24. Ibid., 986.

25. Newton, *The Battle of Seven Pines*, 89.

26. Ronald H. Bailey, *Forward to Richmond: McClellan's Peninsular Campaign* (Alexandria, Virginia: Time-Life Books, 1983), 129.

27. Alexander, *Military Memoirs*, 85.

28. *Official Records*, ser. 1, vol. 11, pt. 1, 772, 787, 825; *Battles and Leaders*, vol. 2, 227.

29. Ibid., 865.

30. Ibid., 957.

31. Newton, *The Battle of Seven Pines*, 78.

32. *Battles and Leaders*, vol. 2, 227.

33. Ibid., 230.

34. Ibid., 226.

35. Ibid., 230; *Official Records*, ser. 1, vol. 11, pt. 1, 767.

36. McHenry Howard, *Recollections of a Maryland Confederate Soldier and Staff Officer* (Dayton, Ohio: Morningside Press, 1975), 150.

37. Shelby Foote, *The Civil War: A Narrative*, 3 vols. (New York: Random House, 1963), vol. 1, 443.

38. I. Werstein, *Kearny the Magnificent: the Story of General Philip Kearny 1815–1862* (New York: John Day, 1962), 213; *Official Records*, ser, 1, vol. 11, pt. 1, 873; W. Clark, ed., *Histories of the Several Regiments and Battalions from North Carolina in the Great War 1861–1865* (Goldsboro, North Carolina: State of North Carolina Press, 1901), 237; Bailey, *Forward to Richmond*, 120.

39. Bailey, *Forward to Richmond*, 138.

40. Wheeler, *Sword Over Richmond*, 225.

41. *Official Records*, ser. 1, vol. 11, pt. 1, 873.

42. Ibid., 1001.

43. Alexander, *Military Memoirs*, 75.

44. Wheeler, *Sword Over Richmond*, 228.

45. Newton, *The Battle of Seven Pines*, 32, 37.

46. Bailey, *Forward to Richmond*, 125.

47. *Battles and Leaders*, vol. 2, 242.

48. *Official Records*, ser. 1, vol. 11, pt. 1, 986.

49. Freeman, *Lee's Lieutenants*, vol. 1, 237.

50. Newton, *The Battle of Seven Pines*, 70.

51. Alexander, *Military Memoirs*, 85.

52. *Battles and Leaders*, vol. 2, 214.

53. Newton, *The Battle of Seven Pines*, 83.

54. *Battles and Leaders*, vol. 2, 215.

55. Newton, *The Battle of Seven Pines*, 83.

56. Ibid., 84.

57. Ibid., 88.

58. Ibid., 101.

59. Freeman, *Lee's Lieutenants*, vol. 1, 253.

60. *Battles and Leaders*, vol. 2, 228.

CHAPTER 6

1. Peter Cozzens, *The Darkest Days of the War: The Battles of Iuka and Corinth* (Chapel Hill: The University of North Carolina Press, 1997), 14.
2. Ibid., 17.
3. Ibid., 23.
4. *Official Records*, ser. 1, vol. 17, pt. 2, 662.
5. Ibid., 685–88.
6. Cozzens, *The Darkest Days of the War*, 56.
7. Ibid., 61.
8. *Official Records*, ser. 1, vol. 17, pt. 1, 121.
9. Patricia L. Faust, ed., *Historical Times Illustrated Encyclopedia of the Civil War* (New York: Harper and Row, 1986), 387.
10. *Official Records*, ser. 1, vol. 17, pt. 1, 66.
11. Ibid., 67.
12. Ibid.
13. Ibid., 118.
14. Cozzens, *The Darkest Days of the War*, 73.
15. Ibid., 74.
16. Ibid., 76.
17. *Official Records*, ser. 1, vol. 17, pt. 1, 121.
18. Ibid., 122.
19. Kenneth Williams, *Grant Rises in the West* (Lincoln: University of Nebraska Press, 1956), 76.
20. *Official Records*, ser. 1, vol. 17, pt. 1, 73.
21. Ibid., 98.
22. Ibid., 119.
23. Cozzens, *The Darkest Days of the War*, 85.
24. Ibid., 88.
25. *Official Records*, ser. 1, vol. 17, pt. 1, 67.
26. Ibid.
27. Ibid., 119.
28. Ibid., 122.
29. Ibid., 70.
30. Ibid., 119.
31. Ibid., 79.
32. Cozzens, *The Darkest Days of the War*, 88.
33. Ibid., 130.
34. Ibid., 102.
35. *Official Records*, ser. 1, vol. 17, pt. 1, 90.
36. Ibid., 112.
37. Cozzens, *The Darkest Days of the War*, 129.
38. *Official Records*, ser. 1, vol. 17, pt. 1, 68.

CHAPTER 7

1. Earl J. Hess, *Banners to the Breeze* (Lincoln: University of Nebraska Press, 2000), 21.
2. *Battles and Leaders*, vol. 3, 6.
3. Ibid., 11.

4. Shelby Foote, *The Civil War: A Narrative*, 3 vols. (New York: Random House, 1974), vol. 1, 719.

5. *Battles and Leaders*, vol. 3, 47.

6. Stephen D. Engle, *Don Carlos Buell: The Most Promising of All* (Chapel Hill: The University of North Carolina Press, 1999), 307.

7. *Battles and Leaders*, vol. 3, 48.

8. Ibid.

9. *Official Records*, ser. 1, vol. 12, pt. 1, 1023.

10. Ibid., 1025.

11. Ibid., 1031.

12. *Battles and Leaders*, vol. 3, 57.

13. Ibid., 61.

14. Engle, *Don Carlos Buell*, 317.

15. Foote, *The Civil War*, vol. 3, 738.

16. Engle, *Don Carlos Buell*, 309.

17. *Official Records*, ser. 1, vol. 12, pt. 1, 1027.

18. Ibid., 1038.

CHAPTER 8

1. E. P. Alexander, *Military Memoirs of a Confederate* (New York: Charles Scribner's Sons, 1907), 286.

2. Ibid., 288.

3. Stephen W. Sears, *Chancellorsville* (Boston: Houghton Mifflin, 1996), 21.

4. Ernest B. Furgurson, *Chancellorsville 1863* (New York: Alfred A. Knopf, 1992), 29.

5. Ibid., 35.

6. Ibid., 56.

7. Ibid., 64.

8. Ibid., 106.

9. Ibid., 111.

10. *Official Records*, ser. 1, vol. 25, pt. 2, 322.

11. Furgurson, *Chancellorsville 1863*, 142.

12. Ibid., 148.

13. Alexander, *Military Memoirs*, 334.

14. Alexander, *Military Memoirs*, 337.

15. John Bigelow, Jr., *Chancellorsville* (New York: Smithmark, 1995), 301.

16. Sears, *Chancellorsville*, 284.

17. Augustus Choate Hamlin, *The Battle of Chancellorsville* (Bangor, Maine: published by the author, 1896), 83.

18. Furgurson, *Chancellorsville 1863*, 169.

19. Ibid., 155.

20. Ibid., 55.

21. Bigelow, Jr., *Chancellorsville*, 246.

22. Douglas Southall Freeman, *Lee's Lieutenants: A Study in Command*, 3 vols. (New York: Charles Scribner's Sons, 1944), vol. 2, 620.

23. *Southern Historical Society Papers*, vol. 30 (1902), 111.

24. *Official Records*, ser. 1, vol. 25, pt. 2, 354.
25. Alexander, *Military Memoirs,* 357.

CHAPTER 9

1. Ed Bearss and Chris Calkins, *The Battle of Five Forks* (Lynchburg, Virginia: H. E. Howard, Inc., 1985), 8.
2. Chris Calkins, "The Battle of Five Forks: Final Push for the South Side," *Blue and Gray Magazine* 9 (5): 8 (1992).
3. Bearss and Calkins, *The Battle of Five Forks*, 6.
4. Ibid., 29.
5. Ibid.
6. Ibid., 46.
7. Ibid., 76.
8. Ibid., 78.
9. Douglas Southall Freeman, *Lee's Lieutenants: A Study in Command*, 3 vols. (New York: Charles Scribner's Sons, 1944), vol. 3, 664.
10. Calkins, "The Battle of Five Forks," 18.
11. Bearss and Calkins, *The Battle of Five Forks*, 77.
12. Calkins, personal communication.
13. Calkins, "The Battle of Five Forks," 22.
14. Ibid., 41.
15. For example: Freeman, *Lee's Lieutenants*, vol. 3, 668; Shelby Foote, *The Civil War: A Narrative*, 3 vols. (New York: Random House, 1974), vol. 3, 870; E. P. Alexander, Military Memoirs of a Confederate (New York: Charles Scribner's Sons, 1907), 591; Bearss and Calkins, *The Battle of Five Forks*, 82.
16. S. Roger Keller, ed., *Riding with Rosser* (Shippensburg, Pennsylvania: Burd Street Press, 1997), 64.
17. *Proceedings, Findings and Opinions of the Court of Inquiry...in the case of Gouverneur K. Warren* (Washington: Government Printing Office, 1883), 472.
18. *Philadelphia Weekly Times,* April 5, 1885.
19. Calkins, "The Battle of Five Forks," 48.
20. *Official Records*, ser. 1, vol. 46, pt. 1, 627.
21. Frederic Cushman Newhall, *With General Sheridan in Lee's Last Campaign* (Philadelphia: J. B. Lippincott and Co., 1866), 93.
22. *Official Records,* ser. 1, vol. 46, pt. 1, 880.
23. Ibid., 893.
24. Ibid., 1105.
25. Ibid., 1130.
26. Bearss and Calkins, *The Battle of Five Forks*, 32.
27. Ibid., 36.
28. Ibid., 40.
29. Ibid., 73.
30. Ibid., 51; *Official Records*, ser. 1, vol. 46, pt. 1, 602.
31. Douglas Southall Freeman, *R. E. Lee: a Biography*, 4 vols. (New York: Charles Scribner's Sons, 1943), vol. 4, 38.
32. Bearss and Calkins, *The Battle of Five Forks*, 93.
33. *Official Records*, ser. 1, vol. 46, pt. 1, 1124.

34. Newhall, *With General Sheridan*, 104.

35. Ibid., 106.

36. Bearss and Calkins, *The Battle of Five Forks*, 103.

37. *Battles and Leaders*, vol. 4, 710.

38. Calkins, "The Battle of Five Forks," 48.

39. Ibid.

Bibliography

Abbott, John S. C. *The Life of General Ulysses S. Grant*. Boston: B. B. Russell, 1868.

Adams, William Taylor. *Our Standard Bearer*. Boston: Lee and Shepard, 1888.

Albright, John. *Physical Meteorology*. New York: Prentice-Hall, Inc., 1939.

Alexander E. P. *Military Memoirs of a Confederate*. New York: C. Scribner's Sons, 1907.

Bailey, Ronald H. *Forward to Richmond: McClellan's Peninsular Campaign*. Alexandria, Virginia: Time-Life Books, 1983.

Bearss, Ed, and Chris Calkins. *The Battle of Five Forks*. Lynchburg, Virginia: H. E. Howard, Inc., 1985.

Beyer, Robert T. *Sounds of Our Times*. New York: Springer-Verlag, 1999.

Bigelow, John, Jr. *Chancellorsville*. New York: Smithmark, 1995.

Botley, Cicely M. "Abnormal Audibility." *Weather* 21: 232 (1966).

Brown, E. H., and F. F. Hall, Jr. "Advances in Atmospheric Acoustics." *Rev. Geophys. Space Phys.* 16: 47–110 (1978).

Calkins, Chris. "The Battle of Five Forks: Final Push for the South Side." *Blue and Gray Magazine* 9 (5): 8–22, 41–57 (1992).

Catton, Bruce. *Grant Moves South*. Boston: Little, Brown and Company, 1960.

Clark, W., ed. *Histories of the Several Regiments and Battalions from North Carolina in the Great War 1861–1865*. Goldsboro, North Carolina: State of North Carolina Press, 1901.

Cooling, Benjamin. *Forts Henry and Donelson: The Key to the Confederate Heartland*. Knoxville: The University of Tennessee Press, 1987.

Cozzens, Peter. *The Darkest Days of the War: The Battles of Iuka and Corinth*. Chapel Hill: The University of North Carolina Press, 1997.

Crouch, Tom D. *The Eagle Aloft*. Washington: Smithsonian Press, 1983.

Davis, Jefferson. *The Rise and Fall of the Confederate Government.* New York: D. Appleton and Co., 1881.

Engle, Stephen D. *Don Carlos Buell: The Most Promising of All.* Chapel Hill: The University of North Carolina Press, 1999.

Fadiman, Clifton. Introduction to *The Collected Writings of Ambrose Bierce.* New York: Citadel Press, 1946.

Faust, Patricia L., ed. *Historical Times Illustrated Encyclopedia of the Civil War.* New York: Harper and Row, 1986.

Fleagle, Robert G., and Joost A. Businger. *An Introduction to Atmospheric Physics.* New York: Academic Press, 1963.

Foote, Shelby. *The Civil War: A Narrative.* New York: Random House, 1963.

Force, M. F. *From Fort Henry to Corinth.* Wilmington, North Carolina: Broadfoot Publishing Company, 1989.

Freeman, Douglas Southall. *Lee's Lieutenants: A Study in Command.* New York: C. Scribner's Sons, 1943.

———. *R. E. Lee: A Biography.* New York: Charles Scribner's Sons, 1943.

Furgurson, Ernest B. *Chancellorsville 1863.* New York: Alfred A. Knopf, 1992.

Garinther, George, R., Joel T. Kalb, David C. Hodge, and G. Richard Price. *Proposed Aural Nondectability Limits for Army Materiel.* Aberdeen Proving Ground, Maryland: U.S. Army Human Engineering Laboratory, Technical Memorandum 3–85, March 1985.

Hamlin, Augustus Choate. *The Battle of Chancellorsville.* Bangor, Maine: published by the author, 1896.

Hess, Earl J. *Banners to the Breeze.* Lincoln: University of Nebraska Press, 2000.

Howard, McHenry. *Recollections of a Maryland Confederate Soldier and Staff Officer.* Dayton, Ohio: Morningside Press, 1975.

Jeans, Sir James. *Science and Music.* New York: Dover Publications, Inc, 1968.

Johnson, Robert Underwood, and Clarence Clough Buel, eds. *Battles and Leaders of the Civil War.* New York: T. Yoseloff, 1956.

Keller, S. Roger, ed. *Riding with Rosser*. Shippensburg, Pennsylvania: Burd Street Press, 1997.

Latham, Robert, ed. *The Shorter Pepys*. London: Bell and Hyman, 1985.

Newhall, Frederic Cushman. *With General Sheridan in Lee's Last Campaign*. Philadelphia: J. B. Lippincott and Co., 1866.

Newton, Steven H. *The Battle of Seven Pines*. Lynchburg, Virginia: H. E. Howard, Inc., 1993.

New York Herald, February 21, 1862.

Olson, Harry F. *Music, Physics and Engineering*. New York: Dover Publications, Inc., 1967.

Orr, Clyde, Jr. *Between Earth and Space*. New York: Macmillan, 1960.

Philadelphia Weekly Times, April 5, 1885.

Proceedings, Findings and Opinions of the Court of Inquiry...in the case of Gouverneur K. Warren. Washington: Government Printing Office, 1883.

Sears, Stephen W. *Chancellorsville*. Boston: Houghton Mifflin, 1996.

———. *To the Gates of Richmond: The Peninsula Campaign*. New York: Ticknor and Fields, 1992.

Southern Historical Society Papers. Richmond: 1876–1959.

Tucker, Spencer. *Andrew Foote: Civil War Admiral on Western Waters*. Annapolis: Naval Institute Press, 2000.

Tyndall, John. *Sound*. New York: D. Appleton and Company, 1896.

Von Borcke, Heros. *Memoirs of the Confederate War*. New York: Peter Smith, 1938.

Werstein, I. *Kearny the Magnificent: the Story of General Philip Kearny 1815–1862*. New York: John Day, 1962.

Wheeler, Richard. *Sword over Richmond*. New York: Harper and Row, 1986.

Williams, Kenneth. *Grant Rises in the West*. Lincoln: University of Nebraska Press, 1956.

Index

A

Alexander, Edward Porter, 37, 41, 73–74, 76, 135–36
Anderson, George, 66–67, 69
Anderson, James Patton, 112, 114
Anderson, Richard H.
  at Chancellorsville, 127–29
  and Five Forks, 145, 148, 158–59
Antietam, battle of, 100, 120
Atmospheric absorption, 14

B

Banks's Ford, Virginia, 127, 129–30, 138, 140
Barksdale, William, 128
Beauregard, Pierre, 38, 42, 46, 50–51, 84–85, 102
Bragg, Braxton
  and Iuka, 85–87
  and Perryville, 100, 102–3, 105–12, 117–20
Buckner, Simon B., 51, 54–55, 58–59, 112, 117
Buell, Don Carlos
  and Fort Donelson, 44–46, 50
  and Iuka, 83–86
  and Perryville, 100–103, 105, 107–12, 114–19
Bull Run
  first battle of, 37–38, 41, 61
  second battle of, 85, 108
Burnside, Ambrose, 120–22, 124–25

C

Casey, Silas, 64, 67, 69, 73
Chancellorsville, battle of, 125–43
Chattanooga, Tennessee, 85–86, 103, 105, 107
Cheatham, Benjamin, 112, 117
Chickahominy River, 3, 4, 63, 66, 72–73, 75–76, 80, 82, 145
Cincinnati, Ohio, 107–8
Condensation, 7–8, 10, 13, 15–16
Corinth, Mississippi, 84–87, 91, 100–101, 103
Couch, Darius, 73, 126, 128
Crittenden, Thomas, 109, 111–12, 114, 118
Cumberland Gap, 106, 119
Cumberland River, 45, 47, 50, 54, 60, 83

D

Davis, Jefferson
  and Chancellorsville, 125, 127
  and Five Forks, 160
  and Iuka, 85, 93
  and Perryville, 105–6
  and Seven Pines, 62–63, 72, 79, 81–82
  and use of the telegraph, 39
Dinwiddie Court House, Virginia, 147–48, 158

E

Early, Jubal, 42, 128, 130, 139–40
Ely's Ford, Virginia, 126

F

Five Forks, battle of, 32, 144, 150–60
Floyd, John B., 51, 54, 59
Foote, Andrew H., 46, 48, 50, 53, 55
Forrest, Nathan B., 59
Fort Donelson, Tennessee, 44–48, 50–61, 83–84
Fort Henry, Tennessee, 45–50, 53–55, 61, 83–84
Fourier, Jean, 11
Franklin, William B., 4–6, 63, 77
Fredericksburg, battle of, 39, 121–22, 142
Frequency, 9, 11–16, 27

G

Gaines's Mill, battle of, 1–3, 5–6, 142
Garland, Samuel, 66, 67–69
Gilbert, Charles, 109, 111–12, 114, 116, 118
Geometrical spreading, 13–14
Grant, Ulysses S.
  and Five Forks, 144–45, 147, 159
  at Fort Donelson, 46–47, 50–51, 53, 55, 56, 58–60
  at Iuka, 83–87, 91–94, 96–101
  mentioned, 61, 103, 105, 107

H

Halleck, Henry
  and Fort Donelson, 45–46, 50, 59–60
  and Iuka, 83–85
  and Perryville, 103, 115, 119
Hardee, William, 50, 110–12
Hearing, 28, 35

172